FREELANCE TRAINING

How to Crack the Freelance Training Business in India

FREELANCE TRAINING

How to Crack the Freelance Training Business in India

Amit Joshi

Indus Source Books

Indian Spirit, Universal Wisdom

Indus Source Books
PO Box 6194
Malabar Hill PO
Mumbai 400 006
INDIA
Email: info@indussource.com
www.indussource.com

Freelance Training: How to Crack the Freelance Training Business in India

First published in India by Indus Source Books in 2017

ISBN: 978-93-85509-05-6

Cover design by Sanskruti Graphics, Mumbai

Printed at Thomson Press India Ltd., New Delhi.

"Dedicated to the Divine force that caressed me during the tough times of my life and pushed me further during the better times; the force that manifested itself sometimes through family, sometimes through friends, and sometimes, sans any medium."

Acknowledgements

I wish to express my gratitude to my Publishers, Friends, and Family.

Special thanks to Senior Trainers Mr. Dharmendra Rai, Mr. Nikhil Desai, and Mr. Vinesh Sukumaran for their valuable inputs and advice for aspiring trainers, which are included in this book.

Contents

Preface

"Give me six hours to chop down a tree and I will spend the first four sharpening the axe."

—Abraham Lincoln

"If I really want to improve my situation, I can work on the one thing over which I have control myself."
—Stephen R. Covey, *The 7 Habits of Highly Effective People*

After spending over four-and-a-half years in the Freelance Training field and having worked with over forty different companies, I gathered the confidence to write this book and guide aspiring and novice freelance trainers in their career. With most of my efforts, trials, errors, struggles, and successes still fresh in my mind, I hope this book can prove to be useful for someone who has just started or is planning to tread in this direction.

At the time I ventured into Freelance Training, I was clueless of what lay ahead of me. The first year was a struggle as I tried different ways to get things rolling and obtain regular assignments. Today, I have reached a level where I am comfortably exceeding my earlier salary, with a potential to grow at a much faster rate in the coming years. In course of time, I made several friends in the training fraternity, many of whom have just made a start in this field along with others who are well established. Some of these novices have approached me several times, asking for either references for work or for tips on how to get more assignments. Moreover, as I started training with several companies, I met many employees who were intrigued and curious when they learnt that I operate independently. Many of them were contemplating such a move, but hesitated to do so as they had no idea of how to go about it. I assume many of the readers of my book are facing the same challenge. Although I regularly help new trainers, I feel that a quick conversation cannot do justice to this topic. There needs to be a structured strategy to tread in this uncharted territory. This book is intended to precisely provide that to the new trainers, or for others who are either planning or dreaming to take the plunge in the Freelance Training market. I have written this book for all those trainers and to-be trainers to help them with the initial phase of their endeavour and take off some pain from their exciting journey in this profession.

As a novice Freelance Trainer, you might have several questions such as: How do I market myself? Where do I find potential clients? How do I enter into a contract with my clients? How do I choose my area of specialization? What are some of the challenges I will face as a Freelance Trainer? and many more. This book covers all these aspects of venturing into a Freelance Training career, right from the scope of training business and assessment of personal skill set, to finding out your own niche etc. It will also help you with all the available options for marketing yourself and creating your own brand.

One of the biggest concerns while taking such a step is managing finance. Hence, I have included a chapter dedicated to managing your finances. Additionally, I have narrated my own personal journey, showing exactly how I did it with all the minute and painstaking details in an effort to give the reader a vivid picture of this exciting career choice. In addition to my own ideas and experience, I have also added the views of top industry professionals from the L&D field to provide the readers with some extra expert guidance. **Digital Resources** through a QR code (see p. 117) have been provided for more in-depth content—videos and soft copies of some material—on certain topics. With that, I feel you will have enough resources at your disposal to refer to while choosing the option of Freelance Training.

I hope that this book instils confidence in my readers to pursue their training careers and eventually helps them succeed.

Chapter 1

Scope of Training Industry in India

There is no doubt that there is immense scope in the Learning and Development (L&D) arena in India. This scope can be easily understood and identified by understanding the dynamics of the skill requirement in industries and the gap between the industry requirement and the current education system.

Of our 1.2 billion population, 54% is under the age of 24, making India the youngest country in the world.

By 2020, it is estimated that the global shortage of skilled manpower is likely to touch 56.5 million, while India is likely to have a surplus exceeding 47 million.

If India is to realize its dream of becoming an emerging superpower over the next two decades, then it is time to do a reality check on our education system and revamp it, if required, to meet the global demand for skilled manpower. There is a mismatch between skill requirement of the world of work and skills imparted by our educational institutions.

The system caters mainly to the needs of the traditional manufacturing sector, which represents less than 10% of the total workforce. The requirements of modern high-tech industries and services sectors as well as those of the unorganized sector are not properly taken care of. Inadequate involvement of stakeholders in the design and implementation of the training programmes has further widened the skill gap.

Considering training from an organization's perspective, there are basically two approaches that organizations have. Many organizations treat training as a continuous activity. They make every manager in the organization responsible for training, which invariably results in learning updates either in technology, methodology, or in behaviour. In some organizations, training is used as a tool to deal with specific problems. In these organizations, training happens only when there is a problem which needs to be solved.

Certain recent changes in perception have done a lot of good to corporate training. More and more skills are taught and learnt, and fewer skills are regarded as inborn.

The change of technology is occurring at a faster pace, rendering skills of today obsolete tomorrow, thus making training and re-training imperative. Globalization has resulted in diversity in lifestyles, attitudes of people, working environment, etc., compelling employees to get trained in various skills like languages, negotiation techniques, communication skills, etc.

Looking at the market, I have realized that there is a lot more opportunity as well as requirement for many more trainers.

Points to ponder:

* Scope of Training industry

What are the areas you are planning to conduct trainings in? (A few broad subject areas are fine. You will be able to further refine your specialization based on the ideas in the chapters ahead.)

Browse the internet and portals like LinkedIn to find out the scope of business in the chosen areas i.e. the number of companies in your city, approximate workforce, training requirements posted, etc.

Chapter 2

Why Freelance?

Most of the readers might be already convinced by the idea of Freelancing over taking up a full-time job. However, for others who are still contemplating whether they should take up Freelancing, it will help if we refresh some of the advantages of Freelancing over a full-time job. Some of the advantages are mentioned below.

You are your own boss: This is the single biggest advantage of a Freelancing career. When I was first contemplating starting a business, I discussed the idea with some of my friends who were already running their own businesses. One of them gave me very valuable advice. He said: "If you are contemplating starting a business, don't do it for money but do it for a lifestyle." Although I was already attracted to the idea of having freedom while working, this advice further reiterated the point. I can also admit that this is the real motivation especially during the initial stages of your Freelancing career, when the money is hard to come by. So what does it mean to be your own boss?

- You are answerable to yourself and yourself only.
- You have the freedom to make mistakes and learn from them.

- You can decide where to focus your energies and what tasks to avoid.
- You can work as per your timings.
- You can take leave whenever you want and for whatever duration you desire.

Although all of these advantages come with their own caveats, they are worthwhile motivators from a holistic perspective about your career.

Even though working independently has several benefits, people avoid it due to the notion of security that a job provides. A general belief is that a job provides more security than a business. Although this is true in the short term, over the long term, it is in fact less secure. Working as an employee makes you dependent on one single company for your earnings, which is quite risky should something happen to the company or to you while working. On the contrary, working as a Freelance Trainer helps you align to multiple clients, thus gaining the advantage of diversification.

Also, being able to work with various companies enriches you multi-fold as a professional in your own field.

Besides, the Indian market is now opening up to take up Freelance professionals. In future, there will be many more opportunities for independent professionals to select a career of their choice.

Above all, in the words of Seth Godin, choosing to be a Freelancer gives you an opportunity to do "Great" work and not the kind of work that you are told to do.

Points to ponder:
* Why do you want to pursue Freelance Training?
* What are your motivators and apprehensions related to the Freelance Training field?

Chapter 3

Working on Your Mindset

"I think anything is possible if you have the mindset and the will and desire to do it and put the time in."

—Roger Clemens

"You can grow if you are willing to feel awkward and uncomfortable when you try something new."

—Brian Tracy

"Press forward, do not stop, do not linger in your journey, But strive for the mark set before you."

—George Whitefield

Before discussing the technical details of how to progress in the Freelance Training business, I would like to discuss some very important mind-set shifts that a Freelancer needs to make. You will have to work on two aspects of your mindset; firstly, your mindset as a Trainer, and secondly, your mindset as a Freelancer.

Trainer Mindset

Staying positive:

This may sound like a cliché. However, it is very important for a trainer to be positive. In general, there is too much negativity and scepticism around, and that's why a trainer should be positive. S/he should positively believe in people's potential, in their capacity to change themselves and develop in their chosen field or profession. A trainer also needs to believe in the effectiveness of training as a tool to solve organizational problems. Though it may not solve all of them, a majority of people's challenges can be addressed and resolved by training. A trainer who does not believe this at heart should leave the profession.

Analytical and calculative:
Along with being positive, a trainer needs to be analytical and calculative. S/he constantly needs to dwell upon the personalities, strengths, opportunity areas of his participants. S/he also needs to constantly evaluate the effectiveness of the training intervention whether it will meet the requirements/ expectations of the operations team/the participants. Can there be something additional done to make the programme more effective?

Think business:
A trainer always needs to look at training as a business requirement, which means it is done with the purpose of solving organizational problems and not just for the sake of doing it. The more a programme equips the participants to learn deeply and apply the learnings in their day to day job, the more effective it is considered. The trainer also needs to be prepared for his programme to be evaluated from the perspective of ROI (Return on investment) i.e. the benefit derived in monetary terms as against the investment made. A programme, however good in terms of participant feedback, is ultimately considered ineffective if it does not generate ROI for the business.

Balancing "expertise" with training ability:
Being a trainer, it is often likely that one gets dragged to go a long way into gathering subject matter expertise, so much so that one often overlooks the ability to train. One must

understand that these are two distinct traits, and one needs to achieve a fine balance between the two. A trainer who has in-depth subject matter expertise but lacks basic presentation skills or facilitation skills is as ineffective as someone who has good facilitation skills or presentation skills but has very poor domain expertise. And whenever s/he looks at improving, s/he must look at developing both of these aspects.

Willingness to learn:
As much as a trainer needs to train other people, s/he must be constantly exploring areas to improve himself and grow. One way of improving your own delivery is just to be exposed to some top quality trainings. You need to have a vision for yourself in terms of where you would like to be in the next five years or over a longer period, and accordingly prepare a list of trainings that you would need to attend to get there.

Freelancer mindset:
Now let's understand the mindset you will need to cultivate as a Freelancer.

Irregular income:
As discussed before, a Freelancer needs to be mentally prepared to live with an uncertain monthly income as against a fixed salary that gets credited monthly in a nine-to-five job. At best, you can plan for quarterly income and compare performance on a quarterly basis. This is a very critical aspect for sustaining in the business.

Investing in your professional development:
We did discuss earlier that a trainer must have the willingness to learn and to upskill himself. Here, I would like to emphasize the financial aspect. All these trainings require an investment to be made, and as a Freelance Trainer, you need to plan for that.

So far, whatever professional trainings you might have undergone would have been the ones that your organization would have sent you for, which means that they were primarily beneficial for the company, and not exactly meant for you.

However, you would have gone for these trainings as they have been provided by the company free for you and there would have been some perceived benefits for your professional growth as well. But, I have noticed that when it comes to investing in one's own self, a typical employee mindset is not able to fathom the need for spending before seeing the reward. This is the most limiting of all mindsets. As a Freelance professional, you will need to regularly invest in your own professional development whether for upskilling yourself, or for marketing, even if there are no immediate financial benefits of doing so. Most of these expenses will not give you direct immediate benefits. Experts say that you must spend around 10% of your revenues for upskilling yourself. You can do so by attending different trainings from senior trainers pertaining to your field or online courses or by reading books.

Living with less:
One other drawback of an employee mindset is the lifestyle addiction because of a fixed income. As you are confident of a fixed income, you will tend to build expenses which are sometimes beyond your actual capacity and much less justified. This soon turns into a vicious cycle which then forces you to look for a higher fixed income and makes you a perpetual employee. On the other hand, when one turns to Freelancing, unless you have a very strong financial backing, you will have to live with far less income for a few months before you make a start. This will require a lot of sacrifice in your lifestyle and is a real test of your grit to make it in the Freelancing world. I personally waited for three years before I could book a car just because I wanted to settle in my Freelancing business more than I wanted a car. This resulted in a lot of inconvenience while commuting; nevertheless, I was willing to live with that. Likewise, you will have to decide what you are ready to give up to manage with limited or no income in the first few months or even a year.

Flexibility:
This trait has more to do with the type of work you choose to do as a Freelancer. One of the disadvantages of working as an

employee is a fixation for job profile. Although it is good to have a clear idea about what role or tasks you would like to perform, such prioritization should not become an obsession so much so that you start considering other tasks as menial or below your dignity. This especially applies to working independently. As a Freelance professional, you will not always get the types of assignments that you initially planned to do. You should, of course, plan to ensure that you do only the kind of trainings or projects which you like, but should also be flexible to do other trainings which come your way just to keep you going, especially in the beginning. In my case, I prefer doing Behavioural, Soft Skills and Leadership Trainings. However, I realized early on that there is a higher demand for Communication Skills Trainings; and my professional background made it easier for me to secure these trainings with the BPO industry relatively easily. I readily took on these assignments till I started getting assignments of my choice later on, which was when I started a bit of cherry-picking. This is one of the reasons I could manage my finances during the initial stages.

In addition to the kind of training assignments, you also need to be flexible with the tasks that you need to perform. As a Freelancer, you will not have any support staff in the beginning which means that you will have to multitask and perform all sorts of roles—right from coordination to content development to raising invoices and following up for payment etc. So, if you are not comfortable with these kinds of tasks, it may turn out to be quite difficult to manage.

Along with the above, be flexible to travel to different cities if need be. This not only will make you available for more assignments, it will also help you gain much-needed exposure.

Besides these, I remember having agreed to even print training material for twenty participants and carrying it to the venue from my place, just because the training vendor had some issues with getting them printed.

Although you can set limits to the amount of flexibility you show, it will certainly make you more likeable to your clients.

Initial Struggle:

"Till you find work, finding work is your main work."

The first 3–6 months as a Freelancer can be quite challenging. Especially in the Indian context, Freelancing is still quite uncommon, hence many people still consider that if you are freelancing, you are essentially in-between jobs, or worse, doing nothing. Even some of your friends or relatives or even family members will ask you to take up a full-time job.

More than what your friends and relatives think about you, what is important is what you think about yourself. Just keep the faith in your own self and pursue your goals.

The main struggle in the initial days is the utilization of time. When I started, work did not flow quickly. So, my day was quite unorganized not knowing what to do. I wasted a lot of time, sometimes surfing the net or reading or trying my hand at some other odd jobs. There was no strategy in place, until one day when it clicked to me that till I find some work, finding work is my work! From then on, I started a structured routine spending most of my time in approaching potential clients via online platforms, or personally understanding their requirements and pitching for business. Very soon, things started rolling and I started getting regular work. Once that happened, there was no looking back. I had crossed the initial hurdle!

Even you will face a similar challenge in the beginning for at least 3–6 months, and my suggestion to you would be to follow a similar approach of planning your days, mostly meeting as many people as possible, online or personally, and keep pitching. I equate it to sowing as many seeds as possible. You never know which seed will bear fruit and give you your first break. I remember a couple of my deals were cracked exactly one year after I first chanced upon them and even forgot about them. All of a sudden I would get a call, and they would ask for my help for their requirements.

Resilience:

One of the hardships in your earlier days, especially if you haven't been a trainer earlier, is the classic chicken and egg situation. You won't get projects until you have experience, and you won't get any experience unless you get some projects to work on. To tell you my story, after approaching a few people who had posted their requirement on LinkedIn, I managed to get an interview call and give a demo session for one of the BPOs. The requirement was regarding a Voice Coach. I prepared for the interview and thought that I could manage it. Instead, when I went for the session, I was asked questions left, right and center, most of which I could not handle. My hands were literally trembling because of nervousness. Not only was I rejected, I think it was so bad that the training vendor didn't even give me any feedback probably fearing that I would breakdown because of that. So, did I give up the idea of training? Of course not. In the words of Sylvester Stallone, ***"You, me, or nobody is gonna hit as hard as life. But it ain't about how hard you hit. It's about how hard you can get hit and keep moving forward. How much you can take and keep moving forward. That's how winning is done!"***

The most important thing I gained from that interview was understanding the client requirements and knowing what they ask in the interviews. I came home and did extensive research on YouTube on the subject, developed a plan on handling these sessions going forward and Lo! The future sessions were much better and were never a hurdle any more. So much so that recently I recorded videos and developed the whole content for voice and accent training for an online training company, and was featured as one of the best trainers on the subject on their portal. What is possible for me, is possible for all of you. So just be prepared for the challenges and take them head on rather than dodging them.

Working with uncertainty:

While working in a nine-to-five job, you have a fixed daily routine and also a monthly or yearly pattern of work, whereas, there is a sharp contrast in this area when you are working as a Freelancer. There is no fixed schedule for trainings unless you are working on a long term contract. In a best case scenario, the dates are confirmed a month in advance. Sometimes, even confirmed programmes can get delayed or cancelled. On other occasions, you might get urgent requests just a day before the programme. You need to be mentally prepared to handle all this. You need to have a strategy about how you would utilize your non-training days, manage in case of urgent requirements, shuffle and adjust your schedule for ad hoc requirements, etc.

Points to ponder:

* Why do you want to venture into training profession?
* What changes will you make in your current mindset to align yourself to some of the mindset shifts discussed in the chapter?

Chapter 4

Skills Required to Be a Trainer

Every trainer has a distinct style of delivering trainings and sooner or later, you will develop your own. One or more dominant skills differentiate one trainer from another. Some trainers are good presenters while others are very good at facilitating. Some are extraordinary story tellers, while some are good at creating compelling content. There are some basic skills that every trainer must possess to become effective at delivering trainings:

- Communication skills
- Language ability, vocabulary, written and oral communication skills
- Presentation skills
- Facilitation skills
- Content development
- Art of using training tools
- Creating energy
- Marketing

You might have questions about the last two traits. However, they are very important, as the more you are able to motivate your participants, the more open they will be to receive your learning.

Marketing, in terms of weightage, has more importance than all of the other skills put together. Hence, whether you like it or not, you will have to work on your marketing skills if you wish to survive or thrive in this business.

Beyond these skills, always remember this great thought from William Ward,

"A bad teacher tells, a mediocre teacher explains, a superior teacher demonstrates and a great teacher inspires."

As a trainer, your highest aim is to inspire your participants to act, to change, and to grow, and you as a Trainer should stand out and lead by example. They should look up to you for any guidance or advice for their personal and professional growth.

Points to ponder:

* What skills do you possess which can make you a good trainer?
* What are your strengths and opportunity areas with respect to the Freelance Training profession, and how do you plan to work around them?

Chapter 5

Knowledge Is Power

Apart from the mindset and skills mentioned earlier, a trainer, especially in the corporate sector, needs to have an understanding of some basic concepts related to Learning and Development. I will just make a reference to these subjects here as there is ample material available on these subjects on the internet as well as otherwise. The readers are expected to research these and get themselves up-to-date with these concepts. Also, these are absolutely basic and essential concepts that a trainer must know, hence, it is not enough if they have just read them once and forgotten about them. These must be engraved in your brains such that you can describe them whenever required. The topics are listed here:

- Pedagogy vs. Andragogy—Difference between Child Learning and Adult Learning styles
- Learning styles—Visual, Auditory, and Kinaesthetic (VAK)
- The Unconscious Competence Model of Acquiring New Skills—The stages of learning from Unconscious Incompetence to Unconscious Competence

- Blooms Taxonomy—It is a set of three hierarchical models used to classify educational learning objectives into levels of complexity and specificity. The three lists cover the learning objectives in Cognitive, Affective, and Sensory domains. They were named after Benjamin Bloom, who chaired the committee of educators that devised the taxonomy.
- Kirk Patrick's Model of Training Evaluation—A standard model for evaluating a training: Reaction, Knowledge, Behaviour, and Results.

Chapter 6

Business Development

Business Development/Marketing/Selling and other synonymous terms pose the biggest challenge for Freelance Trainers. In my conversations with aspiring trainers and existing employees/participants of my programmes, one of the most frequently asked questions is: "How do you market yourself?" or "How do you approach and get clients?" Understandably, these are the questions anyone would have, because, as employees, we are completely cut-off from this aspect of the business. However, it is extremely critical to understand right at the onset, the importance of marketing yourself as a trainer.

Some of the benefits of marketing yourself are:

- Increases your visibility
- Increases awareness of your service offering to your potential clients
- Helps build a healthy pipeline of assignments/projects
- Critical for survival

Now that we have discussed the importance of marketing, let's look at some of the basics of marketing.

Dr. Philip Kotler defines **marketing** as "the science and art of exploring, creating, and delivering value to satisfy the needs of a target market at a profit. Marketing identifies unfulfilled needs and desires. It defines, measures and quantifies the size of the identified market and the profit potential. It pinpoints which segments the company is capable of serving best and it designs and promotes the appropriate products and services."

The entire edifice of marketing is based on four basic elements namely:

- Product
- Place
- Price
- Promotion

Product:

For training purposes, the product will obviously mean your area of specialization. This area has to be chosen with utmost care. For choosing the appropriate area of specialization, it is critical that you introspect and know yourself thoroughly well. Think about your education, professional experience, your strengths, opportunity areas, what ticks you, and what it is that you are excited to talk about. Once you give a deep thought to these aspects, it will be easier for you to pick your area of specialization.

"Only as you do know yourself can your brain serve you as a sharp and efficient tool. Know your own failings, passions, and prejudices so you can separate them from what you see."

—Bernard Baruch

"He who knows others is wise; he who knows himself is enlightened."

—Lao Tzu

While deciding the area of training, one of the most common mistakes Freelance Trainers make is trying to be a jack of all trades. When asked about the training areas at which they are good, they usually end up giving a long list of topics/subject areas. I remember having a conversation with one trainer who was delivering trainings on Aptitude and Quantitative skills to one of the colleges. He said, "I also do trainings for Soft Skills/Behavioural Skills and I train on Six/Sigma and Process improvement as well."

One of the reasons one might do this is to not lose out on training opportunities, as early on it is a challenge to get a constant flow of projects. However, in the long run, this approach proves to be detrimental to your career as it is practically impossible to deliver good quality trainings on a wide range of topics, and sooner or later, your clients will realize this. Secondly, it will be difficult for your prospects to identify with a particular area of training, thus reducing the chances of referring you for any programmes.

One of the other pitfalls, though not fatal in my opinion, is that trainers deliver trainings on very generic areas such as Communication Skills or Soft Skills. Of course, these are routine programmes in most of the organizations, hence always in demand. However, the commercials are very low due to high supply of such trainers in the market. Therefore, although it may be a good idea to start with delivering such programmes, on the other hand, you need to develop some niche areas of training for standing out as a trainer and also to earn higher revenue.

Thus, it is important for trainers to identify one or two areas of specialization as per their liking/passion and pursue their training career in that area. A few questions that you should ask or research before claiming to be a specialist in a particular are:

- Can you name 5 authorities (internationally reputed trainers, authors in that field) in that area of specialization? Eg. Ram Charan, Jack Welch, or Malcolm Gladwell for Management, etc.
- Can you name 10 theories pertaining to that area? Eg. For Leadership: Blake Mouton's Theory, Traits Theory, Situational Theory of Leadership, etc.
- Can you identify 10 skills required to excel in that area? Eg. Communication Skills: Listening Skills, Effective Questioning, Language proficiency, etc.

- Can you identify 10 behaviours that will help someone excel in that area?
- Can you identify 5 jobs that will help you improve in that area?

  Eg. Contact Centre job to improve Communication Skills.

Besides the above reasons for choosing an area of specialization, here is an additional tip. From a marketing perspective, you need to choose an area of specialization for which you are either the first or only trainer in your city or region doing so. The reasoning behind this approach is understood from some great tips given in the book, *22 Immutable Laws of Marketing.* I have included some basic ideas from the book at the end of this chapter. Even then, I would recommend that you read the entire book to get a firm grip on the concepts explained.

Place:

As a Freelance Trainer, you are of course working from home, so there is no question of which place to choose for work. Besides, you will travel to client offices for delivering trainings. As discussed earlier, I recommend that you should be willing to travel to different cities other than your home town to get exposure to different people, cultures, etc.

Price:

Pricing is one of the most crucial aspect of your business and a very tricky one too. A lot of trainers approach me with this question of what commercials to charge for delivering the trainings. I would like to highlight a few approaches to tackle this challenge.

If you are a novice trainer, since you do not have any experience and you are unsure of your effectiveness in solving the clients' problems, you will not be able to dictate the price for your training.

One of the approaches is to give some free demo sessions

which can be a mini version of your full programme. In this session, make sure that the participants gain valuable inputs, and that it is not just a marketing pitch for your complete programme. Once the participants and your clients have realized the value of your programme, you can fix the price of your programme based on the following criteria:

- Competitor pricing for the same or similar programmes
- Global standards
- Time investment
- Material/props required
- Marketing effort involved
- Assistance required, if any, etc.

Although the above steps are quite logical and should be followed as far as possible, I started off with a very simple formula. I simply calculated my per day salary of my previous job, added some buffer to it since I knew that I will not get work on a daily basis, and started quoting that as a price. Whichever company was fine with that readily accepted it, whereas others negotiated a bit, and ultimately we were able to close on a mutually agreeable price. This approach worked well for me initially and helped me survive during the initial struggle.

Also, one should know that there are two ways of getting training assignments:

- Directly from a company
- Through another training company which is a vendor to the direct client

You will notice that whenever you do a contract through another training company, you will obviously receive a lesser amount than that in the first case, as the training vendor will include its margin before paying you. They have some standard commercials which they offer to all trainers and there is very less scope for negotiations. Without doubt, it is a good strategy to get assignments through training vendors at the beginning of your career to gain some experience. Once you have some experience, try getting assignments from direct clients and negotiate the commercials as per the guidelines listed earlier.

One of the other factors that I consider while quoting the commercials is whether it is a short term or a long term assignment. For short term assignments, typically one or two days, I charge higher per day commercials as compared to long term assignments which are typically for 10–12 days.

Also, you should consider the fact that you will be investing some time and effort in the form of pre-training meetings, calls etc. before the actual delivery and therefore the commercials should be increased accordingly. These methods can be good enough for a start. Besides, one must be flexible to change this amount once you start speaking to the clients and get to know the actual commercials offered in the market.

Moreover, as freelancers, you will see some good months and some bad months; for this reason, it is critical that if it comes to your survival in the business, be practical enough to work at lower commercials.

Some other factors you should consider are:

- Whether you need to provide content or just need to deliver client's content, and
- Whether you need to send a programme outline before the training is finalized.

These factors will give you an idea of your time and effort input, and you can modify the commercials accordingly.

Once the commercials are finalized, you also need to clarify the payment terms with your clients and make sure that there is total transparency in this regard.

While we are discussing the commercials, I think it would help if I put some rough numbers in terms of commercials for various training programmes just to serve as a guideline for someone who is starting out completely afresh.

Here is a table which gives you an idea of the commercials offered for different types of programmes when you are empanelled with a training firm:

Sr No.	Type of programme	Training experience	Per day commercials	Expected monthly revenues
For junior level employees with 0-5 years experience				
1	Communication skills/induction training-corporates (Content and TTT provided by the client)	2-5 years	₹ 3000/- to ₹ 4000/-	₹ 45000/-to ₹ 60000/-
2	Communication skills-corporates (content developed by the trainer)	3-5 years	₹ 5000/- to ₹ 6000/-	₹45000/-to ₹ 60000/-
For mid-management level employees with 6-12 years experience				
1	Communication skills, presentation skills	4-6 years	₹ 6000/- to ₹ 8000/-	₹ 60000/-to ₹ 80000/-
2	Soft skills/ behavioral skills– eg. Customer service, people management etc.	4-6 years	₹ 6000/- to ₹ 8000/-	₹ 60000/-to ₹ 80000/-

Note: These are approximate figures based on the current market scenario and subject to change. Also, as these are figures offered by training companies, you can expect a 20%–30% increase if you manage to secure a direct client.

You may also get some long term assignments every once in a while, where the companies may offer you anywhere between ₹ 55,000/- to ₹ 75,000/- per month depending on the requirement and your level of efficiency. Even these are approximate and conservative figures and you will be able to get a very clear idea once you actually start out in this profession.

Promotion:

"Doing business without advertising is like winking at a girl in the dark. You know what you are doing, but nobody else does."

—Steuart Henderson Britt

"In the modern world of business, it is useless to be a creative, original thinker unless you can also sell what you create."

—David Ogilvy

"The business that considers itself immune to the necessity for advertising sooner or later finds itself immune to business."

—Derby Brown, author

Now that you have decided your area of specialization and your commercials, let's discuss the promotion aspect of marketing. There are several ways of promoting yourself. The two main modes of promoting yourself are:

- Personal contact
- Online promotion using social media

Personal Contact:

Through Calls, Personal Meetings or Visiting Forums.

One of the best ways to promote yourself is by meeting people personally or by calling them. The advantage of personal meetings is that your clients get to see you face to face which increases the credibility manifold and quickens the entire process. While promoting yourself through other media, though it may give you a good start, online meetings are generally followed by a face to face meeting.

As a start, try calling your former colleagues or friends and let them know about your plans to start Freelance Trainings. Even I started in the same manner by calling at least fifty of my friends. Out of those friends, one connected me to a person who later on helped me get a long-term assignment. Furthermore, he helped me with some very useful tips when we met.

Besides this, there are several forums for Learning and Development professionals for networking and knowledge sharing, and it will be a very good start for you if you actively participate in such forums. While most of these forums are free, there are paid organizations too, and you can consider joining these based on the value it could add for you.

Some these forums are:

- L&D GLOBAL
- Rishi Gangoly & Dharmendra Rai Trainers Expo: The Trainers Expo is a revolutionary concept in learning & development. Top speakers share their expertise with learners in a series of brief talks. This enables great learning, trainer evaluation and amazing networking. Special offers may be given at the Expo! This has become incredibly popular with 46 Expos done till date and has taken place in Mumbai, Pune, Delhi, and Bangalore. Learners, HR Managers, L&D Pros, Trainers and Future Trainers have found this platform incredibly useful.
- SHRM
- BNI—Business Networks International

BNI: Business Networks International

With over 195,000 members in 7,500 plus chapters worldwide, Business Network International (BNI) is the world's leading referral organization. In 2015, BNI members generated millions of referrals resulting in over $9.3 billion in closed business worldwide. BNI was founded in 1985 by Dr. Ivan Misner "for the primary purpose of building powerful referral networks".

Chapter Format:

- The BNI organization works by creating a group of people from various industries and encouraging regular passing of referrals.
- Each chapter allows one person per occupational

classification, and prospective members must be approved via an application process.

- BNI's philosophy is "Givers Gain". Members are expected to focus on giving referrals to other members to build relationships and receive referrals in return.
- Chapters have specific rules regarding required attendance in order to cultivate the relationships needed to create a comfort level in referring business.
- Chapters track the monetary amount of passed business in order to prove the value of the financial and time commitment.

Website: www.bni.com

My personal experience with BNI has been such that I went for one introductory meeting by paying a nominal fee and could bag an assignment just by attending that one meeting.

When planning to go for these networking events, you need to work on the areas mentioned below:

Visiting cards: Make sure that you have well-designed visiting cards whenever you go for these events. People may ask for a visiting card and not having one may leave a bad impression. Nowadays, it is very easy to get professionally designed visiting cards at very reasonable cost from websites like Printvenue and Vistaprint. You can select a design from a range of options and choose the one that suits your requirement.

Grooming: If you are an established trainer, your grooming may not matter much (nevertheless, I do not know of well-established trainers who are shabbily dressed) but as an aspiring trainer, you cannot afford to ignore this aspect. You might be meeting most of the people at these events for the first time, so you need to leave a good first impression. Ensure that you are formally dressed as you would be for an interview. This would reflect a lot about your commitment and passion.

Elevator pitch: Whenever you meet anyone, the first question they usually ask is, "What do you do?" Of course, you don't want to be completely stumped or fumbling when asked this question. Hence it is imperative that you prepare a crisp elevator pitch (short but impressive introduction) about yourself to leave a good first impression on the people you meet. You can research the internet for tips on how to prepare a good elevator pitch.

Reach before time for such events and optimize the time to meet as many people as you can. Once you have met them, follow up with them over the phone or personal meeting to take your relationship to explore potential business opportunities.

Online promotion using Social Media—Through LinkedIn, Facebook, etc: One of the greatest advantages for present day professionals is the advent of social media and some great professional platforms such as LinkedIn and Facebook. I use LinkedIn extensively for my business and 90% of my business comes through this platform. Here are some statistics highlighting the power of LinkedIn platform.

- LinkedIn has 332 million members and two new users join every second.
- It has 42 million unique mobile visitors per month. This stat is up from 29 million a year before. (This is a 45% increase in just twelve months.)
- The average time a user spends on LinkedIn is seventeen minutes per month.
- 25 million LinkedIn profiles are viewed every day.
- One in three professionals on the planet are on LinkedIn.
- 41% of millionaires use LinkedIn.
- LinkedIn users spend 26% of their time on LinkedIn using the mobile app.
- Geographical reach of LinkedIn: 200 countries and territories.
- Number of LinkedIn users in India: 35 million.

The above stats are more than enough to convince one about the power of LinkedIn. You may ignore it at your peril!

LinkedIn and other social media platforms are great tools to connect with like-minded people and increase your visibility in front of your potential clients. If you would like to use LinkedIn for promoting yourself, then read the following paragraphs carefully and make sure that you implement all of the steps mentioned.

Creating Your Profile

The first step in increasing your visibility on LinkedIn is to create a professional profile. The first thing that your potential clients will do when you connect with them or if they have found you via search is to go through your profile and check if you meet their requirements.

A professionally created profile will give you the following advantages:

- Increased visibility for your role through relevant keywords
- A great first impression
- Details of your work experience, strengths, achievements, etc. so that your clients can decide if they would like to connect with you.

A good profile should have the following features:

Completeness: One of the first things that even LinkedIn rates your profile on, is the completeness. Make sure that all the sections of your profile are filled and that you have not left any of them blank.

Updated: Make sure that you update your profile with the relevant details at regular intervals so that there is no gap in your LinkedIn profile and your actual work experience. This will increase your credibility in the eyes of your clients.

Professional: You need to ensure that your profile looks professional and nowhere should the reader see any hints of casual attitude or shabbiness. A profile with basic errors like punctuations, capitalization, and grammatical errors is a sure-shot recipe for a casually made profile.

Impactful: Besides being complete, updated, and professional, it is also important that your profile is impactful. Remember that having over 30 million subscribers means that there will be many more trainers like you on LinkedIn, and you need to stand out from the others if you hope to get a decent response from your clients. For this to happen, you need to follow the steps discussed.

Filling out a profile isn't difficult, but there are some important best practices you should follow to make sure yours is as powerful as possible:

- ***Add a professional photo***

LinkedIn is a professional site, hence, a casual photo where you are dressed in pyjamas or shorts is not acceptable. If possible, have a professional photographer click your photo and add that to your profile. If not, add the best high resolution photo of yourself where your face is well lit and clear. And smile! Remember, that photo may be your first impression on a potential employer. In addition, if possible, add a photo that shows you in action, as a trainer conducting a session.

LinkedIn allows you to add two photos, a cover photo and a profile photo. Add a cover photo as well. It may be of some session you conducted, or your photo along with some relevant information about yourself, or the programmes you conduct.

- ***Your headline***

By default, LinkedIn populates your headline with your job title and current company, but you don't have to leave it that way. Consider listing your specialty in that section. If you want your profile to be searchable, include important keywords. If that's not a big concern for you, consider getting away from industry jargon to stand out. Try to keep your headline to about 10 words.

Eg.—Corporate Trainer | Soft Skills and Communication Skills | L&D Consultant

Contact details

Although you might have your apprehensions in sharing your contact details on your LinkedIn profile, I would like to let you know that it works. I have received calls on my mobile and direct emails regarding requirements. Hence, if you have a separate business number/email address which you can publicly share, do add that in your profile.

- ***Summary***

Make sure you fill the summary field with detailed information about your background and your achievements. It would be a good idea to check the profiles of the top trainers in the area of your specialization and see how they write. You need not copy their profile, but you will get a good idea about how to write your profile. Again, add as many keywords as possible in your summary to make it searchable. For example, if you are looking for assignments in Mumbai/India as a Freelance Trainer, try to include these words in your summary. You can also add media files, including videos. An introduction video could be a great idea.

- ***Your experience***

Fill this section with complete information about your work experience along with the job description with roles and responsibilities. Highlight any training experience you might have had with each role. You don't need to list every single job you ever had. Instead, only list the jobs that are relevant to your current career goals. You can also add media files to your experience. It's a great way to create a visual portfolio along with your standard resume information.

- ***Other information***

Fill out as much of the profile as possible that includes skills, volunteer associations, education, etc. This is the place to put all the interesting stuff that doesn't fit on your resume, but paints you as a well-rounded individual. If your volunteer experience directly pertains to your job search, put it in as work history so it's up in the relevant section.

Add links to relevant sites. If you have a work-related blog or online portfolio, make use of the three URLs you are allowed on your profile and link to it.

- ***Ask for recommendations***

Do not underestimate the importance of recommendations in your profile. Reach out to past colleagues, managers, and associates and ask that they write you a recommendation. This increases your credibility with your readers. Besides, from a marketing standpoint, it acts as a social proof, and goes a long way in influencing your audience. In addition to asking for recommendations, also write plenty of recommendations for your colleagues and friends. Although hard to believe, it can be a great way of promoting yourself. For example, in your recommendation for your participants, you can start by mentioning that ABC attended my workshop on Effective Communication and I found him...etc. This can be a subtle way of promoting yourself.

- ***Certifications***

Make sure that you add all relevant training related certifications in this section with the details of what that certification is about. These carry a significant weight in the Training industry.

Follow these tips to gain some traction:

Be active

Once you have made your profile according to the guidelines discussed, it is now time to increase your visibility. You can achieve that by being active on LinkedIn. Becoming a LinkedIn member and creating a profile, but not being active on LinkedIn is like having a Mercedes car in your garage, but not driving it. You need to become active on LinkedIn to reap the maximum benefits from your account.

You will have to decide on some minimum amount of time that you will spend on LinkedIn on a daily basis. In the initial days, you may have to spend more than an hour every day. However, once you have done sufficient groundwork, you will need to spend successively lesser time to gain the same amount of output.

Build your network

The most important thing about networking portals is your network size. Remember that online networking is different from personal networking, and the conversion ratios are much smaller. Hence, for you to have a significant output from your LinkedIn account, start with building your network as large as possible. LinkedIn allows a whopping 30,000 members you can connect with, which is more than enough for you to get business from for your entire life. Start by inviting people you already know to connect on LinkedIn. You can also invite people who are not yet on LinkedIn by sending them emails on their personal ids. In the beginning, do not think too much about whether a particular connection is immediately relevant or not. You can think about these questions once you have hit the limit of 30,000. Besides, LinkedIn also makes suggestions to you, based on your profile and your current network, of people you may know. Go through these from time to time and you will surely find people whom you might have worked with and forgotten about. This prompt is based on your current network, which also means that you will appear in the "people you may know" section of more people if you have a wider network, which is one more reason to build as large a network as possible. For the number of connections, think of thousands and not hundreds, and ideally hit the limit.

When it comes to becoming active, start by taking small steps such as liking or sharing relevant updates or links. On your home page, LinkedIn shows updates, articles, links, and messages from members of your network. You can go through these and look for the ones relevant to your field. You may find some really nice and useful articles for yourself. In case you like what you find, make sure that you like or share it. This not only encourages the one who has posted the article, it also increases your own visibility.

Join groups

LinkedIn has numerous groups for all categories and industry types. A free membership allows you to join a maximum of 50 groups. Groups are a great way to build your network and also to find work or business. My recommendation is to join the maximum number of groups. While searching for the groups,

LinkedIn also shows you the group size and how active the group is, i.e. the number of discussions happening in the group. Join groups which have the maximum members and are the most active.

Once you have joined these groups, you can build your network by introducing yourself in these groups. You can also send connection requests to people from your groups who you think might be able to collaborate with you. Some examples of such groups are:

- Groups for IT professionals
- Groups for Trainers
- Groups for Entrepreneurs

Responding to discussions

Once you are a part of an active group, you will see a lot of discussions happening around many topics. These discussions may range from some updates related to the industry, questions on a particular topic or problem, or even job postings/business opportunities. For someone who would like to gain the maximum advantage from his LinkedIn profile, it is a good idea to be a part of these discussions and respond appropriately. The advantages of responding to questions posed in the group are:

1. It increases your visibility in the group.
2. It establishes you as an expert in your field.

As mentioned earlier, you will also find job requirements and business opportunities posted in the groups. So what do you do when you see such a post?

E.g. *"Required Freelance soft skills trainers for a week long assignment in Mumbai."*

More often than not, whenever you see such a post, you will see many people responding right below these posts with comments such as "Interested" or "View my profile" etc. I am not sure how many people with these kind of comments get any response from the poster, unless they have a desperate need for people. But this approach certainly does not stand out among the other responses.

In other cases you will see people responding with a series of questions like, "What are the topics? Which industry? What are the commercials?" etc. Again that is something that can turn off the person who has posted and is not likely to get a response. So if you want to stand out amongst the other participants, you will need to do something different. My approach to these kinds of posts is to personally respond to the post or directly send email with a good cover letter or call the person on the mentioned contact details clearly referring to the conversation on LinkedIn. Even if I have questions around the assignment, the first thing we want is to establish some connect with the person. Once he or she reviews your profile or gets your message, other details can certainly be discussed in the following discussions. Although this approach may not sound radically different, it is certainly not the one of the crowd kind of response and has been pretty successful for me.

Sending messages to prospects

Once you have a sizeable number of connections—minimum 500—you can send messages to your potential clients to introduce your services and seeking business opportunities. While sending these messages, be careful of the timing and frequency and do not spam their inboxes with multiple messages. Also, make sure that your message is drafted in a professional manner giving a clear idea of your services and what you expect from the receiver. Also, keep in mind that the response rate for these messages is very low, maybe 2 to 5 percent, hence it is ok if you do not receive responses to all your messages. Many of your connections might not even be checking their messages and many others might just not be interested. Hence, just be fine with it and move on to pursue the ones who have responded. Some examples of these messages are shown in Section 18H in the book.

Increasing visibility

All the steps discussed so far like being active i.e. liking and sharing relevant updates, joining groups, participating in discussions, etc. will help you immensely in increasing your visibility. This in turn will help in getting more connections which are relevant. So I would recommend once again to do these activities on a regular basis by allocating a fixed amount of time on a daily basis and keeping track of these efforts. These habits will prove to be immensely useful in the long run.

Establishing yourself as an expert

One of the keys to becoming successful in the online world, be it platforms such as LinkedIn or your own personal blog, is to come across as an expert in your field. When people see you as an expert, they will follow you and your articles, thus increasing your popularity. Becoming popular online can give you several benefits offline too. It increases the chances of people approaching you for their requirements, which means more business.

These are a few ways of positioning yourself as an expert in your field:

Content sharing: This is one of the easier ways. In the beginning, if you feel that you do not know too much which is worth sharing or which may add value to the others, you can consider sharing useful content. There would be tons of websites, online magazines and articles which you might find worth sharing. You simply need to share such articles on a regular basis. People do appreciate this and they will look forward for your further posts.

Content curation: A step ahead from content sharing is content curation. The difference is, here you also add your own perspective to the articles shared by you, which the readers might find useful.

Taking part in discussions: There are several forums within and outside LinkedIn where people ask questions or discuss various topics. If you are the type who loves to debate and discuss, then this option is just right for you. You can take part in any of these discussions from your field and let people know your ideas and opinion.

Writing articles: This is the best way to showcase yourself as an expert in your domain. Although, this requires a lot of effort, it is highly fulfilling and rewarding.

Using job sites: Searching for Freelance/Contract assignments is different from searching for a full-time job. Such jobs are quite frequently posted on LinkedIn and using LinkedIn effectively will be of great help in your search. I receive 90% of my business through LinkedIn. However, you should not ignore regular job sites like Naukri.com or Monster jobs for your search. Although most of the jobs posted on these sites are mostly full-time jobs, once in a while even contract opportunities are posted on these sites. Recruiters looking to hire contract employees also look at these sites for suitable candidates.

Your profile on these sites should be complete and regularly updated. You may also consider their paid services for resume development to boost your profile.

The advantages of a professionally designed resume are listed below:

Better searchability: Recruiters, while looking for suitable candidates, search through keywords. While searching, they will look at only the top few resumes which appear through their search. Hence it is extremely important to feature in the top profiles once someone searches for relevant profiles. The resume developers working at these sites have a better knowledge and access to keywords regularly used by recruiters. They include these keywords in the profiles which increases your searchability. Hence, it is worthwhile to invest in professional resume development.

Visual appeal: Once your profile appears in the top resumes, it is also important that your profile is impressive enough to make the cut. Professionally designed resumes have a better visual appeal and hence are more likely to create a good impression.

Therefore, unless you are confident about your own aesthetic sense and your ability to create an impressive profile, it is a good idea to seek professional help. My own resume (added in the Freelance Trainer's Toolkit at the end of this book) is a professionally designed one.

As mentioned earlier, here are some tips from the book *22 Immutable Laws of Marketing*:

Basically, the book says that like other laws of nature, there are some laws applicable to marketing which one simply cannot ignore, and no amount of positive thinking and creativity etc. can help you if you violate these basic laws. The author describes 22 such laws. However, we will look at just a few of them which are relevant to the training business.

Law 1: Leadership—It is always better to be first to market rather than waiting to get to market with a better product.

Law 2: Category—If it is impossible to be first in a category, invent a new category in which you can be first to the market.

Law 3: Consumer's Mind—It is better to be first in the mind of the consumer than to be first in the marketplace.

Law 4: Perception—Marketing is never a battle of products. It is always a battle of perceptions.

Law 10: Division—Over a period of time, most categories will divide into numerous segments, each acting like a category.

Law 13: Sacrifice—You have to actually give up all the choices and focus on one thing in order to achieve anything significant.

Law 17: Unpredictability—Unless you're writing your competitors' plans, the future will always be unpredictable.

Law 19: Failure—Failure in marketing should be both expected and accepted.

All these and other laws mentioned in the book are extremely insightful and can prove to be an important learning for anyone who wishes to excel in marketing their business.

Points to ponder:
* What are the 4Ps of marketing?
* What area(s) of specialization are you targeting based on the ideas discussed in the Product section of the chapter?
* According to your personality, which methods of promoting yourself are you most comfortable with? What are your plans in terms of marketing yourself?

Chapter 7

To Certify or Not To Certify?

As a novice Freelance Trainer, one of the challenges you will regularly face is to establish your credibility with your clients. One of the ways of establishing your credibility is to get some certifications which are recognized in the industry. However, once you try searching for the available certifications, you will be confused rather than being clear about which certifications to get. That's when trainers ask themselves "Should I go for this certification? Is it worth investing the money for this certification?" To answer this question, we need to understand how most of the companies hire Freelance Trainers.

When facing an interview for a Freelance Training position, the first question that the HR asks is whether you have conducted these types of trainings before. So, the answer to whether to get a certification or not is: If you have conducted trainings of the required type, and can comfortably handle them and prove that to the client as well, then certification is not required. However, there are some very specialized programmes which an organization conducts and they look for only certified trainers to conduct those trainings. Besides being required to establish your credentials to the organization, trainings in general are a great learning experience and are a great way to enhance your skill set.

Here are some general guidelines that you may follow to decide whether or not to go for a certification.

Train the Trainer

If you are a novice trainer, you need to do at least a basic Train the Trainer certification. This will give you a good understanding of basic concepts like Adult Learning Theory, Bloom's Taxonomy, Facilitation and Presentation Techniques, and Training Evaluation. However, if you are an experienced trainer and know these aspects of training, a basic TTT might not be immediately required.

Other certifications

While considering other certifications to upskill yourself, I would recommend that you take into consideration the following before deciding to take the certification:

Course content

You need to thoroughly review the content of the programme before taking any decision. It is best to go through a written brochure rather than just the verbal explanation and commitments. You need to check the topics covered and the skill set acquired post the training, and check whether that is something that you are genuinely interested in and whether it is aligned with your long term goals. This is the most important factor in taking a decision. You need not go for a certification only because it is in demand or because it is financially rewarding.

Scope/demand

If you are genuinely interested in the content and skill set offered and if it is in line with your long term goals, you need to do a due diligence about the scope or demand for the particular certification. You can do so by checking on the internet about the demand. You can also look at the training requirements posted by your potential clients and check whether the particular certification is mentioned as a pre-requisite.

The certifying organization

Along with the content, you need to review the credentials of the certifying body. For example, there are several training companies providing Neuro Linguistic Programming certifications and these certifications are provided with a wide range of fees. The concept of Neuro Linguistic Programming was introduced by Richard Bandler and David Lincoln. Hence, a certification done through them would obviously have a higher credibility. Also, check with other senior trainers about the organization before taking a call.

Investment

In addition to the above factors, you need to also consider the investment required to undergo the certification. Not only the financial investment, you also need to consider the time investment to acquire your certification as it may clash with your training schedule and result in some revenue loss. Investment has also to be considered from the Returns perspective i.e.

- How much is the course in demand?
- How much will it help you to increase the effectiveness of your training programmes?
- Would you be able to increase your commercials after completing the certification?
- Is the time horizon for getting the returns immediate or long term?

Your current financial position

This is another crucial aspect that you need to consider while deciding whether to go for a certification or not. You need to see if you have adequate cash reserve to pay for the certification. Most of the times, the returns you get after completing a certification are not immediate, and considering the fact that as a freelancer you might have to face ups and downs in cash flow, you need to plan for the financial aspect very carefully. You might be better off taking a loan for some expensive certification rather than depleting your cash reserve as it may become difficult to manage if you face some rough months in the future.

In addition to the above factors, it is important to understand that merely completing the certification is not enough and does not guarantee results. How you leverage the certification and promote it to your clients is equally, if not more, important. You need to immediately include it in all your profiles and also mention it while introducing yourself. In case of a very important and reputed certification, you may also include it in your visiting card so that your clients know and remember that.

Here is a list of some standard certifications currently offered by various training organizations:

- Train the Trainer—For basic facilitation skills
- Instructional Design—For Content development
- NLP (Neuro Linguistic Programming)
- Psychometric assessments:
- Myers Briggs Type Indicator;
- DISC, etc.

Other specialized certifications:

- Lost Dutchman's Goldmine (LDGM)
- Certified Seven Habits trainer
- Mindmaps, Think Buzan by Tony Buzan

Here is a list of some training organizations providing various trainings and certifications:

- MiddleEarth Consultants: They are the seventh largest HR certification body in terms of number of HR professionals certified, with 1,656 of them in the last one year going through the process of certification. And also the largest HR certifying agency in Asia. Website:http://www.mecindia.in/

• Dale Carnegie: Dale Carnegie & Associates is headquartered in New York, USA, has a presence in 91 countries. It has trained more than 9 million people worldwide in more than thirty languages. Over 400 of the Fortune 500 companies, and successful individuals from Olympic Champions to Corporate Leaders and Heads of States are clients of Dale Carnegie Training.

Dale Carnegie Training India represents the first corporate face of the Training Industry in India. As a company dedicated to Performance Enhancement, it offers "Talent Development Solutions" in the areas of Leadership, Communications, Presentations & Public Speaking, Sales Training, World Class Customer Service, Interpersonal Skills, Building High Performance Teams, Media Training, E-Learning, Executive Coaching, and Profiling & Competency Assessment tools in a variety of formats to suit various needs.
Website: http://www.dalecarnegie.in/

• Bodhih Training Solutions: Bodhih is one of the most sought after organizations in India in organizational development. They have added value to companies such as Microsoft, SAP, GSK, Netapp, Madura Fashion, Gulf Oil, ISRO, Daimler, and IIMB. Bodhih's training systems are built to international quality standards. They are amongst a handful of Indian Companies with the ISO 9001:2008 certification from TÜV SÜD, Germany. Website: https://www.bodhih.com

International institutes:

- IAF—International Association of Facilitators
- ICF—International Coach Federation

Points to ponder:
* Research the internet to identify the certifications available in your area of specialization.
* Chalk out a plan on when you intend to acquire these certifications.

Chapter 8

Getting Started

Having discussed the very important aspects of promoting yourself personally or online, let's understand the next steps once you start getting responses from your prospective clients.

There are two ways of getting work:

1) Directly from a company that wants to conduct some training in their organization

2) Through training companies which conduct trainings for their end-clients and empanel Freelance Trainers to conduct the programmes.

Here are the steps that you will go through to get work through both these modes:

1) Directly from a company that wants to conduct some training in their organization:

- The client approaches you for a training requirement and enquires about your readiness to conduct such training.
- They ask you for your profile and a sample outline of the programme.
- Vis-à-vis meeting with the client which may include a demo/teach-back session to gauge your delivery style.

- If TNI (Training Need Identification) is not done by the client, they might ask you to conduct a TNI and then ask for a proposal.
- The client reviews your proposal and approves.
- You deliver the programme as per the requirement.
- Post-training review of the effectiveness and feedback of the programme.

2) Through training companies which conduct trainings for their end-clients:

- The training company shows interest in working with you.
- They ask for your profile to see if it matches their requirement.
- Telephonic or a vis-à-vis discussion with the training company.
- The training company sends an empanelment agreement to be signed between you and the company.
- The training company then approaches you for relevant training requirements for their end-clients and checks for your availability.
- They may ask you to send an outline for the training requirement, or they may themselves have ready outlines for the requirement. They send the outline and your profile to the client for review.
- The client reviews your profile and the outline and gives consent to go ahead.
- The client then has a telephonic discussion/face to face meeting along with a teach-back/demo session.
- The client gives a final go ahead for the training.
- You deliver the programme as per the requirement.
- Post-training review of the effectiveness and feedback.

The first thing that the companies will ask you for is your resume or brief profile. It is very important to understand the difference between the two and to know what information to include in each.

Trainer profile:
Your trainer profile is a one page brief about your training background, typically including your training experience, training areas, certifications, sample clients served, etc. This is the document that is generally sent to the client by the training company when the client is interested in knowing only your background and experience pertaining to training. I have included a Sample Trainer Profile in the Freelance Trainer's Toolkit.

Résumé: As we all know, a résumé is a detailed 2–3 page document, which, in addition to your training related information, will also have the details of your overall experience, qualification, personal information, etc. In many cases, the client would like to go through your detailed résumé as well, to decide whether you would fit in for their training requirement. You would probably have an updated résumé. However, I have added my own sample résumé in the Freelance Trainer's Toolkit as a reference.

Cover letter: When sending your résumé or profile to the client, it is important to stand out from the crowd. You should know that there might be many other trainers who are sending their profiles as well. In order to stand out and to make a good first impression on the client, you should always include a cover letter/mail while sending your résumé or profile. This letter should briefly talk about your overall experience, your interest towards the requirement and how you would be the right fit for the requirement. I have also included a Sample Cover Letter in the Freelance Trainer's Toolkit section.

Referring back to the steps mentioned, once your résumé is screened and subsequent discussions are done, the training vendor will sign an empanelment agreement with you which also includes NDA (Non-Disclosure Agreement) clauses. You can find a Sample Empanelment Agreement in the Freelance Trainer's Toolkit.

If you are empanelled with a training vendor, most of the

pre-training tasks like sending out proposals, Training Needs Analysis, etc. and even content development (for some of the clients) is managed by the vendor, leaving only the delivery to the trainer. However, if you manage to get some interest from some direct client, you will need to engage with the clients to understand the requirements, a possible demo session, Training Needs Analysis, and sending out the proposal along with the programme outlines and session plan.

Sending proposals: A sample proposal is included for your reference in the Freelance Trainer's Toolkit.

Points to ponder:

* What are your short term and long term goals in terms of number of Training Hours, Students Trained, and Revenue?
* What are the main elements of a Proposal?
* What are the key components of a Course outline?
* What is the difference between a Trainer profile and a Résumé?
* Exercise: Prepare at least 5 course outlines, session plans, and demo sessions in your chosen area of training.

Chapter 9

Delivery Excellence

Once you have bagged an opportunity to conduct a workshop for your client, it is crucial to do your best and exceed the expectations of the clients with your delivery. An excellent delivery involves two critical aspects i.e. Content and Presentation. Let us understand these aspects in detail.

Content

To come up with powerful content for your training, it is important to know the content development process. The ideal process for designing content is the ADDIE model.

The **ADDIE model** is a framework that lists generic processes used by training developers. It comprises five phases:

- Analysis
- Design
- Development
- Implementation
- Evaluation

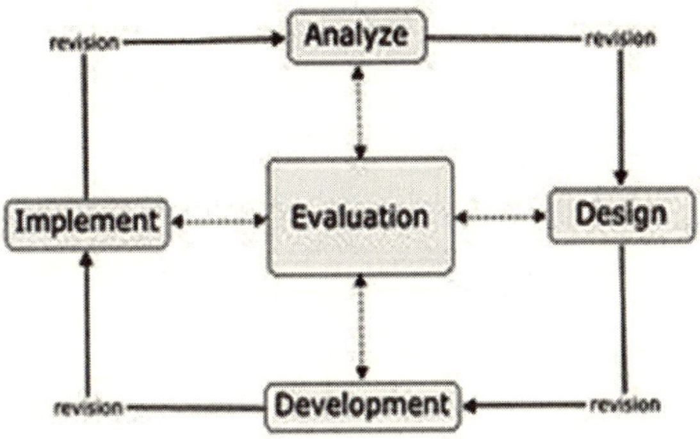

Phases of ADDIE

Analysis phase

The analysis phase clarifies the training problems and objectives, and identifies the learning environment and learner's existing knowledge and skills. The questions that the analysis phase addresses include the following:

- Who are the learners and what are their characteristics?
- What is the desired new behaviour?
- What types of learning constraints exist?
- What are the delivery options?
- What adult learning theory considerations apply?
- What is the timeline for project completion?

Design phase

The design phase deals with learning objectives, assessment instruments, exercises, content, subject matter analysis, lesson planning, and media selection. The design phase should be systematic and specific. *Systematic* means a logical, orderly method of identifying, developing, and evaluating a set of planned strategies targeted for attaining the project's goals. *Specific* means each element of the design plan must be executed with attention to details.

Development phase

In the development phase, developers create and assemble

content components blueprinted in the design phase. The content is then reviewed and revised according to feedback. Usually, your client will expect you to provide or be prepared with the following for the training programme:

***Participant guide/manual*:** This will have the content which the participants are supposed to refer to during the training. It must have adequate provisions for assessments, quizzes, activities, and the reference material that they need to follow. The content should be organized in a logical flow and aligned with your presentation so that it becomes easier for the participants to understand and implement the learnings.

***Power-point presentation*:** This is the presentation that the trainer uses during the programme. It is very important for the presentation to be classy and impactful for the programme to be effective. You can use relevant images to increase the aesthetic value.

***Other elements*:** In addition to the above, one should also include relevant videos in the programme from time to time. Videos are a great way to break the monotony caused by continuous PPT (Powerful Presentation Techniques) presentation, and also to reinforce learning in an interesting manner. Activities are another way to keep the participants engaged and to make the programme lively. A programme should have an adequate mix of relevant activities at regular intervals during the programme. As a thumb rule, after every 5 slides, I add either an activity, quiz or a video to break the monotony and to keep the participants engaged.

The other aspect you need to understand about the content is whether you need to share your whole content with the client i.e. PPT, videos, activity sheets as well as the participant manual, or just the participant manual. This depends on the agreement you have made with your client and you should quote your commercials accordingly.

Note: Some pure content development assignments will also require you to add trainer notes to the PPTs or prepare a separate facilitator guide in word format for the trainer to refer to, which will have details of what the trainer is supposed to say or do during each of the slides.

Implementation phase

The implementation phase develops procedures for training facilitators and learners. Training facilitators cover the course curriculum, learning outcomes, method of delivery, and testing procedures. Preparation for learners includes training them on new tools (software or hardware) and student registration. Implementation includes evaluation of the design.

Evaluation phase

The evaluation phase consists of two aspects: formative and summative. Formative evaluation is present in each stage of the ADDIE process, while summative evaluation is conducted on finished programmes or products.

The evaluation is done at four levels as per Kirk Patrick's Model of Training Evaluation. Here's a brief about the model:

Donald Kirkpatrick, Professor Emeritus at the University of Wisconsin and past President of the American Society for Training and Development (ASTD), developed a 4 level method of evaluating the effectiveness of a training programme.

The four levels are:

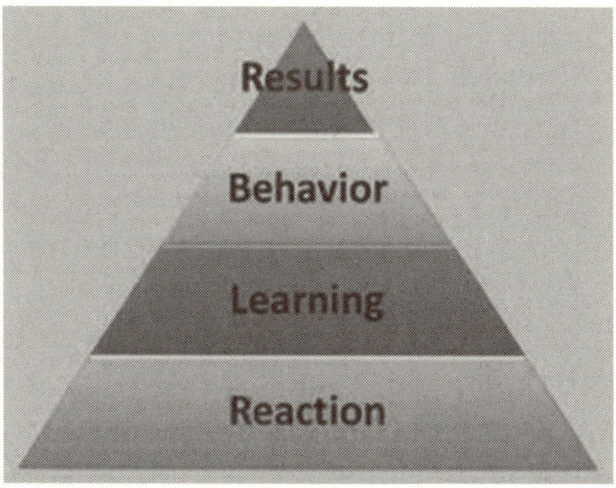

Level 1: Reaction

This level measures how your trainees (the people being trained) reacted to the training. The idea is to capture their feedback about the instructor, the topic, the material, its presentation, and the venue.

It is important to measure reaction, because it helps you understand how well the training was received by your audience. It also helps the organization to improve the training for future trainees, including identifying important areas or topics that are missing from the training.

Level 2: Learning

At level 2, organizations measure what the trainees have learned, and how much their knowledge has increased as a result of the training. This is captured by way of quizzes, pre- and post-assessments etc.

It is important to measure this, because knowing what your trainees are learning and what they aren't will help you improve future training.

Level 3: Behaviour

At this level, organizations evaluate how far the trainees have changed their behaviour based on the training they have received. Specifically, this looks at how trainees **apply** the information.

However, just because behaviour hasn't changed, doesn't mean that trainees haven't learned anything. Perhaps, the environment was not conducive to apply the knowledge. Or maybe they've learned everything that was taught, but they have no desire to apply the knowledge themselves.

Level 4: Results

At this level, organizations analyze the final results of the training. This includes the outcome that the organization has determined to be good for business, good for the employees, or good for the bottom line.

Although, ideally, all of these steps should be followed for developing and implementing an effective training programme, it is also important to understand how it happens in a practical scenario. In case you are empanelled with a training company as a consultant and are conducting a programme on their behalf, they will provide the content for the programme and also train you on it. In other cases, the client for whom you will ultimately deliver the training programme will train and certify you on the content. You will be selected to conduct the programme based on your performance during the certification.

In some cases, even if you are empanelled with a training company, you will be required to provide the training content. In those cases, the training company sends you the requirement they receive from the client in the form of an email and you need to reply with a training outline that you propose to conduct. This is then reviewed by the training company and the client, and confirmed depending upon their comfort with the outline. In most cases, the time duration for this is extremely less, hence there is a struggle to keep up with the deadlines. It is therefore easy to have some rough outlines ready for some standard programmes that you are planning to conduct. This will help you to meet the timelines as per the requirement of the client.

Presentation

Your presentation will decide the success of your programme and will determine whether you will receive further assignments from the client. Hence, you need to ensure that you do an outstanding delivery of the programme. Here are some tips to make your programme engaging and to make sure that you receive great feedback:

Preparation: You need to ensure that you are thoroughly prepared with your content. Not only should you be prepared with the content that you have in your PPT, you should research in depth about the subject beyond what is included in your PPT.

It is said that your content should be 40% in the power-point and 60% in your head. With this amount of preparation, you will be equipped to answer questions effectively, giving valuable insights to the participants.

***Grooming*:** Keep in mind that during the training programme, the participants are not only paying attention to or receiving the content, but also observing you as a person. They want to see you as a person to look up to and probably follow. Hence it is paramount for you to not overlook your grooming, and to project your best image. It is said that people make a perception about someone in the first 7 seconds, hence the saying "First impression is the last impression". To create a good first impression, you should be well-dressed from top to toe.

***Reach before time*:** While conducting your programmes, you might get so busy with the preparation that you might be tempted to spend more time at home doing your last minute preparations for the presentation. However, it is in your best interest to avoid such temptation and reach early. Reaching the venue before time is the first step to ensuring a smooth delivery. You should reach the venue at least 30 minutes prior to the start time. There are quite a few advantages of reaching early:

- You get adequate time to relax and prepare for your delivery.
- You get time to get well-acquainted with the venue, right from the light switches, projector, remote and other controls to the breakout area, restrooms, etc. These tiny bits of acquaintance can prove to be vital to keep you less hassled and more composed during the programme.
- There is a psychological advantage of reaching early; the one who reaches first owns the territory and whoever follows enters his or her territory. This gives a huge boost to your confidence and reduces anxiety.

Here are some additional techniques you can use to engage the audience during the delivery:

Present the big picture: As a trainer, in addition to covering the content of the programme, it is also important to sell the programme. Adult learners are always eager to know the big picture or WIIFM—What's in it for me—for any programme. Your role as a trainer is to emphasize how the programme will help them in performing their day to day job better as well as the long term benefits for their career. Once they are convinced of these aspects, you are guaranteed to get the attention and participation from your audience.

Tell a story: How much ever people grow up, they are always interested in listening to a story. Include as many relevant stories as possible in your presentation to drive home your points more emphatically.

Share personal examples: In addition to stories, you should also share your personal experiences wherever possible. This gives greater credibility to what you are saying and engage your audience further.

Ask questions: Questions are a great way to involve the audience and to test their understanding of the concepts discussed. Hence, it is quite useful to ask some pointed questions from time to time during your presentation.

Show a video: The internet is flooded with loads of interesting and impactful videos on numerous topics. You must make use of such videos to engage your audience. It is an easy and effective way to engage your audience besides giving you a much-needed break from speaking continuously during the programme.

Establish a personal connect: This is also a great indirect way of engaging with the participants especially during long duration training programmes. Make it a point to sit with different participants during the off-training time i.e. lunch time or refreshment breaks etc. Discuss a bit about personal or professional life without sounding too intrusive. Such informal discussions can indirectly boost the participation and engagement even within the classroom.

Make sure that you implement maximum elements from the above in your presentation to make it impactful and effective.

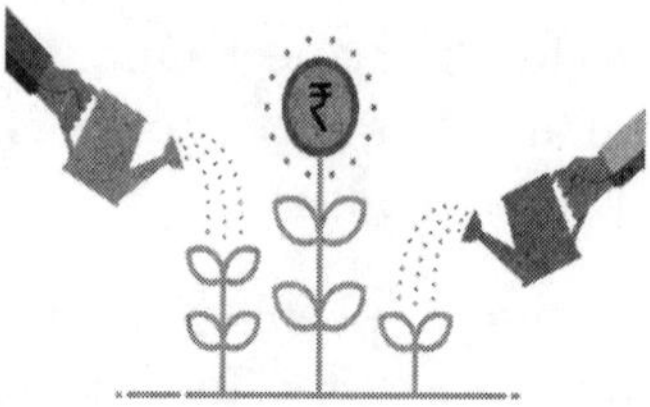

Chapter 10

Finance Management

"If money management isn't something you enjoy, consider my perspective. I look at managing my money as if it were a part-time job. The time you spend monitoring your finances will pay off."

—Laura D. Adams

"When it comes to money, ignorance is NOT bliss. What you don't know CAN hurt you."

—Sandra S. Simmons

Being in the freelancing business, how far a trainer manages his finances is the most important aspect of his professional growth. It can literally make or break his or her career. The biggest drawback of a nine-to-five job from the finance perspective is a fixed salary that gets credited at the end of every month. Though it looks and feels safe and secure, it is extremely limiting and, in fact, damaging, as a person starts viewing financial success or failure only from the paradigm of fixed monthly income and a slow but linear growth. A person becomes completely risk averse and addicted to a fixed monthly income and is extremely uncomfortable with uncertain monthly income even of an overall higher amount.

We can discuss at length about the drawbacks of a fixed nine-to-five job and the real risk in being an employee. But it is not the point here and there are several other books which throw light on this topic. Hence I will discuss only the tactics of finance management for a freelancer.

As a start, you can work on the below aspects of Finance Management.

- Goal Setting
- Deciding your Commercials
- Tracking your Income
- Filing returns

Goal setting

Goal setting is one of the most crucial aspects of your finance management. It takes a great amount of self-discipline to establish challenging goals and then consistently work towards achieving them especially as a freelancer. As an employee, we are thrust with goals from our seniors which are set as per the department, or the team targets, and we are then made to work hard to achieve them. As a freelancer, you are independent! Which means there is no one to pressurize you to set and achieve your targets. This puts all the onus on you to set your own goals. Being absolutely new to the business, you might find this a daunting task as you have no idea what can be considered as a reasonable target. For a beginner, you can consider beating your own salary in the near future and set your targets accordingly. You may set some targets for the next six months to a year, as being new to the field, you do not know the income potential and may want to review your goals frequently in the beginning.

Tracking your income

Once you start getting assignments, it is very important to keep track of all your work and the income generated. You may also want to track the source through which you got that particular assignment. This will not only give you a clear visibility of your earnings, but also gives you an idea of which sources are working best for you, so that you can plan to put additional efforts for marketing yourself through those channels for future work. I keep a regular track of all my work including the smallest assignment. I would like to share a template which you can use as a reference. You can review and use a similar template to track your work as well.

Revenue

	2015 - 2014	2016 - 2015	
Corporate			0
Personal			0
Other contracts			0
Total			0

Hours

2015 - 2014	2016 - 2015	
		0
		0
		0
		0

No. of participants

2015 - 2014	2016 - 2015	
		0
		0
		0
		0

0 0 0

Sr No.	Month Year	Date	Name of the company	Program details	No of Participants	Hours	Revenue	Traning Company	Source

Similar details can be tracked for personal contracts.

Trainings attended

Sr no.	Date	Title	Duration	Investment

Trainings to attend

Sr no.	Date	Title	Duration	Investment

Pipeline:

Sr no.	Company	Programme	Approx Revenue

Filing returns

Tax payment and planning: This is one aspect that most of the trainers I have met are not very particular about. Most of them just do not file their IT returns. Filing your IT returns has two benefits. Firstly, it will help you earn your refund in case TDS (Tax Deducted at Source) has been deducted from your earnings and you have legitimate expenses to show to claim refund. Secondly, having a well maintained IT returns track record will increase your credibility as a professional. This is the first thing that is asked for when you try to secure any loans.

For filing your returns, you should know that all Freelance Trainers come under the ITR (Income Tax Return) IV category which is different from a normal salaried professional. Under this category, you can show valid expenses which include marketing cost, salaries paid, depreciation including car, computers, trainings attended and many others. You must seek the advice of a competent Tax Return Preparer before filing your returns.

Invoicing and payment: These above aspects, if well taken care of, will ensure that you have a smooth journey in terms of finance management, and consequently allow you to focus on your core pursuit which is training. In the end, remember that it is your dream and do not let it go because you had a few tough months from a financial standpoint. Any business, even freelance business, is a long term game and takes minimum 3 years to settle and to see some visible results. Hence, be patient and keep trying until you are able to earn to your satisfaction. Also, keep in mind that you are starting a new career altogether from scratch, so just compare it with your earlier career option and reflect on how long it took for you to earn a significant income. Therefore, you must be willing to put in at least half of that time span to see fulfilling returns.

Points to ponder:

* What are your short term and long term goals in terms of number of training hours, students trained, and revenue?
* What commercials per day do you plan to charge for your sessions?
* What is the basis of your calculations?
* What are the benefits of tracking your income, invoices and payments?

Chapter 11

Overcoming Setbacks

When you are in business, not all days will be good. Even if you are an established trainer, there will be lean patches or rough months and you might even get some negative feedback for your programmes. It happened to me with one of my regular clients. I was working with a major ITES (Information Technology Enabled Services) company for more than seven months when they asked me to present before a panel for re-certification. To everyone's surprise I got rejected in that session whereas I had been conducting trainings for that company for a while. Besides, I was earlier certified to conduct trainings for their senior employees. This incident was quite shocking and I was a bit worried about the future. However, as it happens when you have been in this business for a long enough time, within just a few days, I got a long term assignment from another company which I did for a month and later I bagged a 3 month assignment from a large MNC. Following that I got one of the largest, and very highly paid, assignment with a giant MNC. To sum up, setbacks are bound to happen; all you need is to hold your nerve, keep the faith and go on pursuing. Things will not be as difficult as in the beginning, as you have already seen and overcome tougher times.

Surviving tough times:

"When the going gets tough, the tough get going."
Here are some strategies that will help you to sail through the tough times.

Acceptance

Start with the mindset that you will have to endure some temporary lean patches. First and foremost comes "Acceptance"—to accept that it is absolutely fine to go through these phases, and that work flow and earnings in a freelance profession are not linear and regular as they are in a nine-to-five job. If you had been an employee earlier, this is the most difficult thing to do. We are too used to getting fixed monthly income, and the moment there is some interruption, we start thinking that something is drastically wrong, and added to that, we start imagining all sorts of gloomy future scenarios. The best way to tackle this mental disturbance is to divert your mind to do something to change the situation rather than just worrying about it or thinking of quitting.

Manage finances wisely

Cut short on spends by eliminating expenditures which are not urgent and restrict them to only the most necessary ones.

Use credit

Although it sounds counter-intuitive to use your credit card, I recommend using it and leveraging some credit from your credit card if you foresee a short lean patch. In case you are anticipating a longer one, you can also avail of a loan as it comes at a cheaper interest rate, albeit, for a larger amount.

Take some courses

If money is not a concern, having some time off can also prove to be a blessing in disguise, as it can provide you with some much needed time to upskill yourself, which you normally would find hard to get when having a tight schedule. Keep a ready list of trainings to be attended and which are aligned to your long-term goals. As and when you have some time, attend these and upskill yourself. This can also prove to be a good way of diverting your mind from the worry that sets in because of a lean period.

Side hustle

One of the other things you can do is to work on some alternative source of income just to support yourself during the tough times. In my case, although I do mostly corporate trainings, I conduct personal coaching at times for some clients, especially when the corporate training business is slow.

These tips should come in quite handy to overcome the temporary tough times and remember: **Never Give Up,** because in the end, **"Tough times never last but tough people do".**

One of the other setbacks in my opinion is stagnation—doing the same stuff with similar clients for a long time without changing or growing. This, in my opinion, is a bigger setback than a temporary lean patch. It is said that **the biggest enemy of Greatness is Goodness**. As a freelance professional, your growth is completely dependent on you and the amount of initiatives you take. Hence, it is your responsibility to constantly keep yourself updated with latest trends, doing additional courses, certifications and thus sharpening the saw. This has to be done at regular intervals at a rapid pace. This will give you an edge over the competition and prove to be immensely useful in the long run. As a trainer, you need to value learning, and this will be demonstrated by the initiatives you take in upskilling yourself.

Content creation:

You can also utilize this time to write articles/blogs or create online courses. I too created an online video course for an online training company which I now market to my audience and earn additional revenue.

Chapter 12

Words from the Veterans—Advice from Senior Industry Professionals

Dharmendra Rai

Dharmendra Rai is Mumbai's first Mind Map Trainer and has conducted 260 Mind Map seminars for Executives of Many Fortune 500 Cos, IITs, IIMs, Harvard Business School, Johns Hopkins, Oxford, and London School of Economics (LSE) Alumni. He was ranked # 1 in an International Creativity Test organized by Tony Buzan & Chris Griffiths, ThinkBuzan in Dubai.

Dharmendra Rai has 15 years' work experience with companies like Morgan Stanley, Alliance Capital. Last Position—National Sales Head, Benchmark Mutual Fund, now Goldman Sachs.

He is trained in Lateral Thinking by Edward de Bono, Nobel Economics Prize Nominee. He is an NLP (Neuro-Linguistic Programming) Master Practitioner, endorsed for NLP by Sue Knight, one of the global pioneers in NLP and author of *NLP at Work*. He is a mentor to over 30 start-ups in areas of business strategy, marketing, innovation, learning & sales at

Zone Start-ups.

He is one of the Most Connected People on the Planet; LinkedIn: 44,500 + DIRECT Connections; FB: 5,000 Connections and has also appeared on CNBC, Times of India, DNA, Zee Business and Channel V. In addition, he joined the elite list of TED x Speakers, not just once but four times on Creativity, Mind Mapping and Invisible Selling.

Q. What are your views on the scope of training in India?

A. India is an evolving market and only sheer sweat of quality trainers can grow the market. Professional trainers need to make training interesting and result-oriented. They need to market themselves and their services constantly. That is a terribly wanting thing in India. More than 90% of trainers are parasites i.e. they are there only to earn money and not contribute anything in return. They can offer no useful content and they cannot market their concepts and themselves. They are people who are under the delusion that training is an easy business with a lot of money in it. Also, they want ego gratification by being the guy in the room everybody listens to. This at least is what had drawn them to the profession. They enter the profession and go nowhere but to save face, don't give up the tag of trainer. Such people taint the profession and affect the credibility of the training profession.

Q. What are the essential qualities of a trainer?

A. 1. He should be very passionate about his subjects.

2. He should be very passionate about marketing himself and his concepts.

If he has passion for his subject and no marketing skills he will die frustrated and unknown.

If he has no passion for his subject and possesses only marketing skills, he won't go far.

Q. What are some challenges one may face as a Freelance

Trainer and how can one overcome them?

A. The biggest challenge is that most people in India do not realize the importance of training. They will realize it only when they lose their jobs and businesses. They need to be scared into believing this. Also freelance trainers don't understand branding and marketing, and are not willing to work hard enough to make their careers successful.

Q. Any other advice/recommendations/tips you would like to give to aspiring trainers?

A. Come in for passion not for money. There is very little money in the training business in India though things are getting better.

Nikhil Desai

Nikhil Desai is an International Speaker, Motivator, and Trainer for the last twenty-five years. He is passionate about enabling people to excel in their personal and professional lives.

He received a LIFETIME ACHIEVEMENT AWARD at the WORLD HUMAN RESOURCE CONGRESS 2016. Delegates from all over the world attended this conference.

Nikhil Desai's organization "The Centre for Excellence" has been honoured in the list of the fifty Most Valuable Consultant Companies.

Nikhil Desai has appeared on television and radio in India, New York, California, Philippines, South Africa and Oman.

Nikhil is the only speaker and trainer in the world who has the combined strengths of an MBA from USA, business acumen through his own business enterprises, a qualified corporate yoga practitioner for more than twenty years and has twenty-five years of experience in speaking and conducting training programmes. This wealth of experience enables him to share rich ideas and experiences with the audiences during his sessions which are very interesting, interactive, and impactful.

Nikhil Desai has delivered presentations and conducted

workshops at various national and international events and forums.

Q. What are your views on the scope of training in India?

A. Our educational system does not produce graduates who are work ready. Hence the need for training in India is greater than ever before. In today's competitive times, a trained workforce is going to be the most important competitive edge of an organization. Research has shown that soft skill training is very important in the performance and productivity of success of an executive working in an organization.

Q. What are the essential qualities of a trainer?

A. I believe the following seven qualities are very important for a trainer to possess:

1. Have an ability to learn quickly.
2. Know their subject matter well.
3. Have empathy, and a desire to make others learn.
4. Have excellent communication and presentation skills.
5. Be lively and enthusiastic.
6. Be able to involve participants in activities.
7. Be receptive to feedback.

Q. What are some challenges one may face as a Freelance Trainer and how to overcome them?

A. Some of the challenges for a trainer can be:

1. Not enough work especially in the beginning.
2. Companies offering lower training than before since the number of trainers has increased, but the market has not increased in proportion due to the slowdown of the economy.

There will be many other roadblocks and challenges along the way. A trainer can overcome them only with dedication, patience, and persistence.

Q. Any other advice/recommendations/tips you would like to give to aspiring trainers?

A. Any trainer must decide why he is in this profession. If it is ONLY to make money, there is a likelihood of failing. If the trainer is passionate about making a difference in the lives of others, then success will surely come soon.

Vinesh Sukumaran

Vinesh Sukumaran has several years of people development experience across industries. He is seen as an empirical consultant for organizations like McKinsey, Hewlett Packard, Daimler, The Indian Institute of Management, and Coca Cola to name a few. He is the Director and Principal Consultant of Bodhih, a Bangalore based Training and Organizational Development Consulting firm.

Vinesh Sukumaran's work is about learning, self-development, and self-expression. He has helped individuals find more meaning, be more engaged in what they do and experience greater happiness in life.

While Vinesh Sukumaran has a background in both Mechanical Engineering and Neuro-Semantics, his real expertise lies in the understanding and application of Human Behaviour and Neuro-Linguistic Psychology in Self Development. He is a member of the International Association of Facilitators, and is certified by both the International Society of Neuro-Semantics and the National Federation of Neuro-Linguistic Psychology.

Q. What are your views on the scope of training in India?

A. Training as a field is still very nascent in India. And there are some reasons for that.

1. Even today, there are organizations that don't have a training department or which don't have a formal training structure internally. That is one clear indication that we are still very nascent in that field.
2. Secondly, we actually have the youngest population in

the world, even compared to countries like US and China. This young population will become useful only if they are well-trained, and well-equipped. So, for the size of people that we have, it's a huge ordeal and there is a lot of work that needs to be done in the field of training. Therefore, there is straightaway a possibility and opportunity which lies in the country.

3. Thirdly, if you walk into any of the bookshops in any part of India, you will hardly find a handful of books on training in comparison with places like Singapore, where, though small in size, they are loaded with books for training, accessories, and equipment for training etc. This again indicates that there is a lot of scope and work that needs to be done in the area of training. I think there's a bright future for anybody in the next ten years who wants to enter into training; even for someone who wants to start a fresh career without any background in training, they can still do a great job. There's enough of the pie for everyone.

Q. What are the qualities required for a trainer?

A. One thing I have constantly been telling people is that don't get into training because you see somebody else doing well, somebody else being successful in it; likewise, don't get into training because you feel it's an easier job to do, or you tried other things and now let me also try training. This is to tell you what it's not. It's not a field for passers-by. For the number of people who get into training, there's an equal number of people who also get out.

Q. So what are some qualities of a trainer?

A. Keeping in mind the trainers whom I met who are successful and are excellent trainers, one big quality is, PASSION. One has to enjoy doing it. I think this is very fundamental, because if you don't enjoy doing it, you will not do it well. One might say that this is true of any field, but I think it's particularly true of training. Because you have a direct impact on people's life, you better be doing it in a fashion that's motivating and encouraging.

Secondly, there is this constant battle of, whenever you tell someone that you are a trainer, they are going to ask you, what are you a trainer on? There's a need to become an expert in an area. So, that is another big prerequisite. You have to be so good in an area that if somebody wants to learn, they need to learn it from you. Even if you can pick something very small e.g. just become good in one thing like curing of phobias. If you want to become a good coach, become good at curing phobias. So if anyone comes to you with any phobia, you can fix it. Do just one thing really well, you can expand that into other areas. Likewise in training, you have to pick up some small area where you know everything about it. You can answer questions about it, feel strongly about it. You have to be definitely good in one area. If I have to pick one more thing, it's an extension of the first two things that I told you, but it's really about walking the talk. I think, India specifically, and the world in general, lacks trainers who walk the talk. Lot of trainers who run programmes on making money and being successful are not successful themselves. So it's important that you walk the talk. You first apply what you learnt in life and once you succeed in it, that itself will take you much further as a trainer than any of the other things. These are some of the things that will give you a stronger foundation. Besides these qualities, there are other things like communication, presentation abilities, even sensitivity to participants, or being just a nice person. These are some things that add value as a trainer.

Q. What are some of the challenges they may encounter, either in the beginning or even later on in their career?

A. I will answer this in two parts.

In the beginning, one challenge which (I meet a lot of Freelancers, either through our workshops that we conduct or people who want to ask questions and get clarification) is not training specific but a Freelance related is, you get into a field where suddenly you don't have a fixed income. How do you handle that? Also, not just handling it but handling it without getting desperate.

Secondly, there is the challenge of getting into a thinking that I will live an easy life, or I will just go and make some money. (People think) I met this person who earns 1 lakh a day, he just does that and then nothing else. What they don't realize is what the person must have done to come to that level. That is definitely one challenge thinking that it is an easy life.

The third challenge which comes later on, is of **Self-motivation.** If things are not going your way, it is very difficult to keep yourself motivated and to push yourself harder. Accordingly, find ways to motivate yourself. Another big challenge is **Learning**. It is one reason why many Freelancers fizzle out and take a full time job later on, because they don't learn new things, and suddenly they are not in a work environment. Many times you are training somebody because you are slightly better than them, at least in the area in which you are training. So you are constantly getting the feeling that I know better than them and not exposed to an environment where there are people much better than you. Therefore you stop learning and become complacent as there's no real motivation to learn something else. If you stop learning, if you stop innovating, you take five programmes, you know what's going to happen from start to end, keep repeating that, it could work for you but that's danger. It's just a matter of time you get tossed out of the business.

Fourthly, Trainers reaching a plateau and not knowing

how to move to the next level in terms of income, calibre, etc. It is very clear when you are working in an organization, you have a clear roadmap i.e. if you are a Manager, then you become a General Manager, then you become a Vice President etc. Making a roadmap for your self is the challenge. It's important for you to keep that in mind (and there's not going to be one in front of you). So, you need to create one which is motivating enough and not one which you can easily meet and then hate yourself for meeting it.

Another big challenge is that a trainer should not be just sharing knowledge (that's another big problem in the industry). A trainer should build competence. I think the best training centres we have in the country today are the driving schools because when you go in, you don't know how to drive a car. When you come out, you know how to drive a car at least 90%. There might be a 10% gap and you might buy a new car and bang it somewhere. But by and large, they are great training centres, because you can do something which you couldn't do earlier. There is a tangible and demonstrable change in the person's ability or behaviour. This should happen at the end of a training session, otherwise you are just missing the plot. There are many books teaching "don't worry, relax, don't be jealous," etc. But how many people actually follow that is the question and that's why training exists in the market—to build ability.

The last thing which I want to mention in the challenges is that people should stay. Just stay long enough, keep learning new things, developing your programme, going out and delivering it, and just stay there. Don't run into a full time job because you have to pay your bills and don't have enough money and suddenly your income is stopped. Just stay. You have to try it for some time before it really works for you and this is true for any field. People don't have the horse power to stay and try it for some time, and run away from it and later never do it again because they have failed. They think that it's a flop area and they are not going to make it. One must have the patience and perseverance till they attain the green pastures.

Additional advice

One thing to keep in mind is that it is a great idea to move towards one area of specialization. You don't have to be a trainer who can train in all areas. You are better off becoming a domain expert for a couple of reasons. The first reason why someone would reach out to a Freelance Trainer in spite of having an in-house training department is, because you have some expertise which they don't have. The term domain expert means an expert. So, instead of trying to do a little in all areas, you pick one area and become really good at it, meaning you should rarely meet someone who is better than you, who has gone deeper than you in that subject, both from a knowledge perspective and the skill enhancement perspective.

Secondly, people need to enter the field realizing that it is not an easy field, but it is a tough field to be in. It is a mistake people make thinking "I wanna just become a writer", and they quit their jobs and they start writing. It is not easy to write a book, it is not easy to become popular. Therefore, it is not easy to make a career as a writer. Even Salman Rushdie, a British-Indian novelist, quit his job only after his first book became popular. Training is a field like that and it should be treated like that; enter the field realizing that it is a tough game. And because it is a tough game, be prepared to face it with that level of toughness. People should not listen to anyone who is saying, "It's an easy thing, you can just chill out and work many days from home etc." All that is true but also you might get only one-tenth of your income into the bank, so they should see that.

Besides, training has a lot of poor talent as well, so a person who wants to get into training should not listen to people who could not succeed at it. People will tell you, "Don't make that mistake, don't quit your job, it's a lousy field," etc. But you should realize that just because somebody is making one lakh per day, you will do that immediately; and just because somebody was a loser in that field, you are not going to do that. You are who you are and you need to gauge that and enter the field with that sensibility. It is a field where you have to take a call by yourself and proceed. It is a tough field but a great field to be in, and if you are clear about being in it, you can do well, succeed, have a very satisfying career, make a lot of money, and spend a lifetime of learning and many other perks.

Also, a trainer should be able to wear multiple hats. Sometimes he should build ability, at times be a coach and take people to the next level, sometimes be a mentor and guide to the people to get to where he has gotten. Occasionally he should be just a teacher, sharing knowledge. You should know when to do what.

Chapter 13

How I Did It

Before you read any further, about me, I would like to clarify as to why I included this chapter. The purpose of this chapter is not to brag about myself or to market myself. The purpose is to give the reader a comprehensive background about myself including my education, career, strengths, the industry I worked for, the kind of job roles I performed and the kind of trainings I attended etc., which helped me later in my career as a trainer. A combination of these moulded my personality and my skillset. The readers are expected to similarly reflect on their own careers and draw comparisons to my story to find out trainings, work experiences, and skillsets which can help them in their training careers.

Education

I did my schooling from Mumbai and was amongst the top rankers in my class. I had a strong liking for languages (especially English) and Science. Besides academics, I used to very actively participate in extracurricular activities like debates and elocution competitions and won several prizes in my school for these activities. I also regularly represented my school for such competitions and won prizes at the inter-school level as well.

Post-school, I took up further studies in the Science stream and completed my Engineering in Instrumentation in 2001 from Mumbai University. Even during my engineering days, I actively took part in extracurricular and creative activities and was well-known for my performance in these activities.

Professional background

I started my career in the BPO (Business Process Outsourcing) industry, as an advisor for an Outbound Telemarketing process for an international BPO. As the job involved talking with American customers, I was provided with some excellent training in **Communication Skills, Voice & Accent, Selling Skills and Call Handling Skills** before we hit the operations floor. Our trainer, Ronald James, was a Canadian and did a great job, keeping us all engrossed in his training. He had fantastic observation skills which he demonstrated in one of the off-class conversations he had with us as he pointed out individual traits of the participants from a batch of eighty-plus participants. Apart from equipping me for my job, the training also left me impressed and inspired and probably ignited that little spark and inclination for the training profession.

Post-training, I took calls talking to and convincing American customers for various services for credit cards. I started off as an average performer, but after about six months, although I was amongst the top sellers in my process, I was never number one. However, in terms of quality, I was the best and was awarded several times. One of the traits that I was often complimented for was that I sounded extremely natural and conversational as opposed to many others who sounded robotic on calls. Although I did a good job on calls, my eyes were always set on rapid growth to very senior levels within the company. I would always compare the growth path of my managers and aspire to beat that. Having said that, I also did not want to work all the time as an employee and had a secret ambition to start something on my own in the future.

After a year and a half, I got my first break as a Client Servicing Executive. The role involved managing client accounts and being the face of the company for our clients. It involved interacting with the senior management in our company and our clients for daily/weekly/monthly and quarterly reviews. This gave me great exposure to managing the process and understanding the business side of it. It was quite challenging to meet and exceed the expectations of the clients at all times. I grew a couple of ranks in the same department in about two years and became Assistant Manager Client Servicing. After working for five years in the organization and three years in the client servicing department, I got bored of the monotony of the job and started looking out for opportunities. It took a while to hunt for opportunities as this was the first time I was looking out for a change. However, with some trial and error, and with the help of the services of job portals, I was able to get a change as an Operations Manager in a domestic BPO. This was my first role at the managerial level in the operations department. Nevertheless there was a distinct difference in the functioning of a domestic BPO as compared to an international one and I found myself a misfit in the organization. I left the organization in six months to take on a position as Operations Manager with an international BPO for their back end Data Entry process. Here, I spent two years managing an extremely complicated process with very tight timelines. In fact, that was the most challenging role of my career. Unlike Voice processes, Data processes have their own challenges and have to be dealt with differently. Hence the role helped me acquire the skills required to manage back end logistics processes. Besides, the organization that I was a part of was a Learning Organization with a lot of focus on Learning and Development. Special trainings were arranged throughout the year for all levels of employees to help to them do their jobs well and to help them grow. Some of the trainings I attended were—Management Development Programme, Six Sigma Greenbelt Training, and various other short modules pertaining to Team Management and Process Management.

These trainings were quite helpful not only for my immediate job and overall growth, but they also provided me the exposure which proved to be helpful to me as a trainer. After spending 2 years in that company, I moved on to join as an Account Manager, and later Process Manager in the Global Service Center of the world's largest container shipping company. There, I managed a team of sixty people including four team leaders. My team used to handle Document processing and Mainframe system updates for all end to end documents generated for our client, which was a Supply Chain Management company. Even in this firm, I got an opportunity to attend some top quality trainings on Management and Leadership development conducted by international training companies. These trainings also inspired me to think in the direction of moving to training as a full time career option.

By this time, I had spent over nine years in my career and had successively grown a dislike for the monotonous nine-to-five job. There were several reasons for this dislike, major ones being—monotonous work (regardless of the job profile), lack of creative space, office politics, and lack of freedom. This was when I started taking concrete actions in the direction of my long cherished dream of starting something on my own. I did some research and took a franchise of an English communication skills training institute in Mumbai. I chose the franchise route as I had no prior experience of running a business; hence, I thought that this would be a good option to gain some learning from an already established institute. Also, starting a completely new firm would have required full time commitment which was difficult for me at that time. In hindsight, I feel that the decision was taken in haste and there were several flaws in my approach. Nevertheless, it was a learning experience and I had to take such a leap at some point of time. I managed this franchise parallel to my job for a year by visiting it on weekends and by just supervising during weekdays. This, again, is not an ideal approach for managing your business. At this point, I remember the advice given to me by one of my friends when I was starting out on my entrepreneurship journey. "You cannot run a business on weekends," he said. "At some point, you will have to commit yourself fully to the business." I found it quite difficult and tiring to manage both my job as well as my business. In spite of that, I did not have the courage to leave my secure job and the regular monthly income it gave. The final push to commit myself fully came rather unexpectedly. There were some changes in the management because of which my immediate manager changed. My relationship with the new manager was already strained, and this change worsened the situation. Soon it came to a point where I could no longer take it, and decided to quit my job in December 2012. I could have tried to search for another job at that time, but I gathered some courage and thought of giving a try to my business as well as to try my hand at pursuing my corporate training dream. There was quite a bit of pressure from my friends, well-wishers, and family to reconsider this decision. However, I had made up my mind. I had no clue nor any concrete plan of how I was going to succeed in this adventure, but just had an inner belief that it will succeed. Another practical justification was that if I didn't succeed, I always had the option of securing a job.

Amidst a lot of turmoil, stress, and multiple thoughts, I somehow managed to hold my nerve and started out in this journey. I remember the first day very vividly, when I first chalked out my goals in terms of what I wanted to achieve financially and overall in the next few months and over the long term. On subsequent days, I started calling my old contacts to spread the word out, a couple of which resulted in some headway. I also started using LinkedIn aggressively at that time. I sent almost 200 messages to my contacts to seek some guidance or possible training opportunities, out of which one clicked much later. I joined training-related groups on LinkedIn to look for opportunities and started following the discussions happening there.

Parallel to this, I was also looking into my franchise more dedicatedly and it picked up quite well during that time. But I was not getting any proper direction in the Corporate Training business. Meanwhile, I came across a few opportunities for Voice & Accent training. Since I was targeting Behavioural trainings, I did not pursue them seriously. As I could not see many opportunities for Behavioural trainings, I decided to start out with VNA and Communication skills training opportunities. I immediately got an opportunity to meet one training vendor, who eventually scheduled a teach-back (demo) session with one client for a training requirement. As referred to earlier, I was not quite prepared for this demo session and did very badly, thus losing out on this opportunity. On getting back home, I thoroughly researched the questions she asked and the training topic. Consequently, I did well during other interview opportunities and started getting these Communication skills and Induction training opportunities quite regularly. Meanwhile, as a result of my earlier efforts of contacting my friends, I got in touch with a very senior contact with a reputed educational institute and signed a long-term contract with them. By this time, I started getting regular training assignments from other companies as well, mostly for communication skills. Although this was not my chosen field, I enjoyed this new role and continued for a few months. I had not done any certifications initially. During the first six months of my freelancing journey, I came to know about the "Teach India" initiative. I thought it would be a great opportunity to get some exposure in training while also helping some underprivileged students. As a part of this initiative, I got trained by the British Council which proved to be extremely helpful in the future. The Teach India initiative was a great experience, full of learning for self as well as teaching. One of the best things about the training from British Council was that it made the process of teaching English language a very enjoyable process.

My franchise which had picked up earlier, took a down turn again towards the end of 2013, while I started getting steady assignments for Corporate Trainings. Hence I decided to discontinue with the franchise and focus solely on Corporate Training. Later, I signed a couple of long term high paying contracts which gave me good financial stability as well and a feeling that I had finally **ARRIVED.** Gradually I started getting core Behavioural Training assignments for senior staff which had always been my priority. I keep on upskilling myself through various other trainings and certifications i.e. Train the Trainer, Instructional design, and a few more, and look forward to moving on to progressively challenging assignments. I am also working on establishing a stronger brand for myself and eventually conducting open workshops on some niche topics. I am as fresh and enthusiastic as I started out on my first day, and also more confident, and I have better clarity about the course of action. I strongly believe that the best is yet to come.

Points to ponder:

* Write a brief about yourself including your qualifications, work experience etc. highlighting the skills acquired and the strengths and opportunity areas.
* Why do you want to venture into the training profession?

Chapter 14

Open Workshops

Along with your corporate trainings, you can also look at conducting open workshops in niche areas for your audience. Although there are no constraints to when you can start doing open workshops, I would recommend that you get some experience in conducting trainings before you start open workshops. There are some clear benefits of open workshops which include:

Increased revenue potential: Once you have learned the knack of acquiring a reasonable number of participants for your workshops, your income can literally multiply manifold as compared to corporate trainings.

Freedom and flexibility: The content for your workshops is completely your prerogative and hence you have complete freedom to include or exclude as per your choice.

Brand value: If you are regularly conducting workshops, it adds immense value to your brand which of course has significant long term value.

Along with these benefits, there are some challenges in conducting open workshops which need to be kept in mind:

Marketing: One of the biggest challenges is the enormous marketing effort required to market your workshops and to attract a regular stream of participants for your workshops. This may be particularly daunting if you do not have marketing experience. You need to have established your brand and should have a sizeable number of followers before you dive into this area.

Logistics: If you are conducting workshops on your own, all the arrangements, right from the projector, the seating arrangements and food to participant materials, etc. have to be taken care of by you, which may be quite daunting.

In spite of these challenges, there are many successful trainers who conduct workshops on a regular basis which suggests that there is a sizeable training market which can work wonders for the ones who dare to give it a shot!

In case you are planning to conduct open workshops, there are some portals which help you promote your event for free. I have mentioned a couple of them below:

www.eventshigh.com
www.meraevents.com

Points to ponder:

* What are the topics on which you can conduct open workshops?

Chapter 15

Online Training

"Trainers won't be replaced by technology. They will be replaced by trainers who are willing to use technology."

— Jane Bozarth

We are convinced of the scope of, and rewards from, the training business. However, there is one drawback in this profession, and that is scalability.

If you are a corporate trainer, or are conducting open workshops, there are obvious physical limitations to the number of people you can reach out to. However, modern technology has made it possible to tackle this challenge.

There are possibly thousands of online courses and hundreds of platforms available (many of them for free) which allow you to create and market your courses, tests, etc. If you are a creative and tech-savvy trainer and are able to create engaging courses, then this is the right medium to tap. With the number of internet users multiplying by the minute, online learning and gamification of learning will be the future of learning, and the ones who have tapped these channels will gain the massive returns offered by these resources.

Some of the portals offering online learning platforms are

Udemy, Wiziq, and Classmarker, etc. Here is some basic information about these portals:

Udemy

Udemy.com is a platform or marketplace for online learning. Udemy provides a platform for experts of any kind to create courses which can be offered to the public, either at no charge or for a tuition fee. Udemy provides tools which enable users to create a course, promote it, and earn money from student tuition charges.

Udemy has made a special effort to attract corporate trainers seeking to create coursework for employees of their company.

As per Udemy reports on its homepage, it has served over 10 million students, and offers more than 40,000 course alternatives.

Website: www.udemy.com

WizIQ

WizIQ is a web-based platform for anyone and everyone who wants to teach and learn live online. Teachers and students use WizIQ for its state-of-the-art virtual classroom, to create and share online educational content and tests, and to connect with persons having similar subject interests.

WizIQ lets you produce your content online and convert it in a shareable format, with minimal effort. You can make your content semi-permanent, easy to put on blogs, and embeddable as objects and links.

Website: www.wiziq.com

Points to ponder:

* Online Training/Learning:
  What kind of online courses can you develop?
  Research the different online platforms and their plans on the internet and find out which will work best for you.

Personal website

One additional tool to increase your online presence and to aid your marketing efforts is to have a personal website. There are several advantages of having your own website. Let's understand a few of them.

1. **Searchability**

   Nowadays, prospective employers and recruitment agencies take advantages of the internet to do the initial search for job applicants' information. They want to know more about the applicants, their skills, passion, and life. Having a great website will greatly increase the chance of being selected for an in-depth interview.

2. **Professionalism**

   Whatever you do—work or hobby related—people will perceive you as more professional than if you had not had website.

   The same thing applies to having your own custom email connected to your domain and website. It looks much more professional to use your custom email than doing a business using Yahoo, Gmail, or other such emails.

3. **Accessibility**

   You can connect all your social media accounts to your website. By doing this you maximize your chance of having people notice you.

   Also, if you are looking for a job, you can create your online resume with portfolio of your works and send it to different job portals. It is then much easier to find work. In fact, it makes the work find you rather than the other way around.

4. **Passion and knowledge**

   Passion and knowledge are two pillars for you to succeed in your career. They are also the traits most sought after by clients. Your website provides the best platform for you to show would-be clients the topics that interest you. You can create your true brand through the topics you choose, the style of writing, the design and usability of the website. Though free hosted blogging platforms like Blogger.com and WordPress.com also provide you the same channel for free, your personalization options and control are often much limited. Your website and blog can show the best of you!

Company registration

At a slightly later juncture in your freelancing career, you should also consider moving from working as an individual freelancer to operating as a registered company. Some options for company registration are:

1. Proprietorship or One person company
2. Partnership firm, or
3. Private limited company

Some of the advantage of registering a company are:

- Limited Liability: Registering as a company restricts the liability on the person and transfers it to the company.
- Legal Status and Corporate Identity: Registering your company also establishes your legal status and identifies you as a corporate entity. This lends you greater credibility while dealing with companies and increases your chances of securing business from larger and established firms.
- Helps to build a Brand for your company.
- Easy access to loans and funds from Banks and Financial Institutions.
- Quick decision-making and flexibility in management.
- Tax saving.

Chapter 16

Pre-prep Before the Plunge

Having known all the different aspects of becoming a Freelance Trainer, right from the mindset to the skills, 4Ps i.e. Product, Price, Place, and Promotion, the Empanelment process, and Delivery Excellence, it is now time to sum up everything and break it down to concrete steps to start on this exciting journey. For this, I recommend you to follow the RIPPED approach. This is explained below.

RIPPED approach:

Read/Research/Reflect: This is the first step in starting out on your journey. You need to read and research about your chosen field of training, whether it is Technical i.e. IT, Finance, Banking etc. or Soft skills, Behavioural Skills, Communication Skills, etc. Your research should also involve talking to as many freelance trainers as possible to get more information about the business.

Identify: As a part of this step, you need to simultaneously reflect on your strengths and interest areas, envision your training business, and establish your goals in this business.

You should have reasonable clarity in terms of your career path, your financial goals for the next few months or a year, and clearly document them in a diary or in Excel. Since you are venturing into the freelance world, it can be difficult to have a very clear picture of your career as against a full-time job where there is a clear visibility of career options/career ladder/ designations/job roles etc. However, you need to apply yourself and your research and chalk out your plan as vividly as possible. These steps are extremely critical, and you will be required to perform these steps every now and then during your freelancing career.

Prepare: Once you have done your research and identified your area of specialization, it's time to start with your preparations. You need to prepare the following to get started:

Trainer profile—One page (Refer sample profile in the Freelance Trainer's Toolkit).

Detailed résumé—2 to 3 pages (Refer sample résumé in the Freelance Trainer's Toolkit).

Outlines—Prepare some programme outlines for the programmes you wish to conduct (Refer sample in Freelance Trainer's Toolkit).

Proposals—Prepare a standard proposal template in case a prospective client asks for it (Refer sample in Freelance Trainer's Toolkit).

Visiting cards—Prepare your visiting card to hand over during your personal meetings and networking events.

Social media profile—Prepare an impressive LinkedIn profile based on the guidelines mentioned earlier.

Promote: The next step is to actively promote yourself. Start joining Trainers' Networks and other relevant forums and network with as many individuals from the industry as you can. Become active on social media as per the tips mentioned earlier, and start approaching prospective clients and training companies.

Engage: The next step is to engage with the leads generated from your efforts and close.

Deliver: The last and the most important step is to deliver the programme as per the requirement. Make sure you do an outstanding job which can ensure ongoing business.

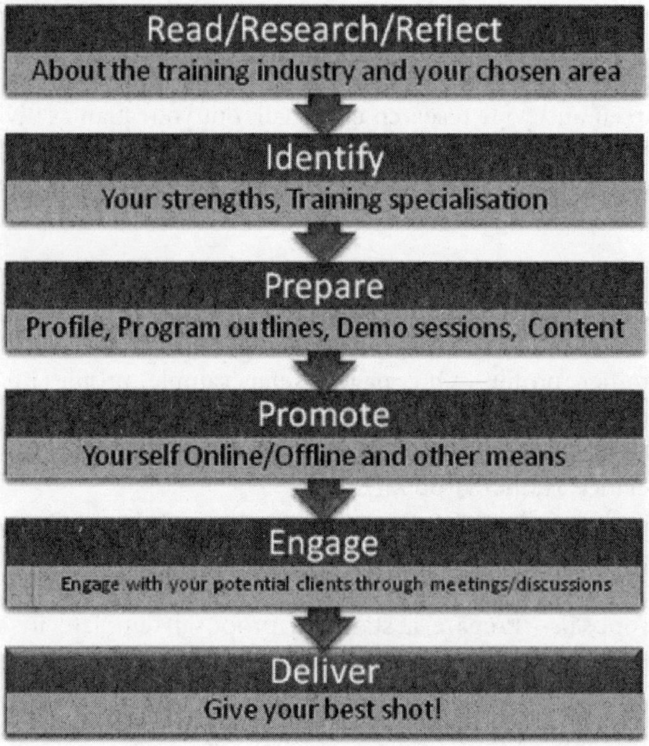

Chapter 17

Conclusion

By now, you would have got a vivid picture of the Freelance Training business and also perhaps realized that it is not easy to make the transition. I sincerely hope this book has thrown enough light on this business for you to be confident enough to make the first move in this direction. I have a few expectations from my readers which I would like to convey in this concluding note. The expectations are as follows—Act, Refer, and Spread.

Act: You would have noticed that this book is all about action. I have shared practical tips and actions one needs to take to work in this field. These are not theoretical ideas but concrete steps that you can implement immediately. Hence, I urge you to not over-reflect on the ideas, but instead, get your hands dirty by trying out these steps. You might not get it right the first time or something might not work for you. However, don't give up, and give it another try. Sow as many seeds as you can and something will work for sure. If you have decided to act, DO IT NOW! Don't postpone it for later. You may never know when you get caught up in life, may even forget about it and remember again when it is too late. I am sure you don't want to be in a situation at a later point in life when you sit back and think that you should have done this.

You may not even want to do things in the same sequence as mentioned in the book and that's fine as long as you do something. So, whether it is updating your LinkedIn profile, printing your business card, attending some conference, or just meeting some members of the training fraternity, take some step, and I am sure that it will take you a long way.

Refer: The second thing I expect from my readers is to keep this book as a handy manual and refer to it time and again. The reason behind this is that you may not fully appreciate or understand the relevance of some of the content in this book immediately. However, when you practically start implementing things, you might get stuck at some point or the other and may not remember that the solution might be mentioned in this book. Hence, refer to it time and again, and you may receive some newer insights.

Spread: My third expectation from the readers is that if you have liked the ideas and if some of the ideas have worked for you, please spread the word and help other trainers too. There are abundant opportunities in the market for all of us to work and grow together. So don't worry about the competition. I have realized that every time I have passed on a reference or some assignment, it has only helped me in the future.

In the end, I would like to leave you with some lines of an inspiring poem which I read in the autobiography of our former President APJ Abdul Kalam—*Wings of Fire.*

"For all your days prepare
And meet them ever alike,
When you are the anvil, bear –
When you are the hammer, Strike."

All the best for your exciting journey! May God bless you with success and satisfaction!

—Amit Joshi

Chapter 18

Freelance Trainer's Toolkit

A: Consultant's Agreement

(BETWEEN ABC AND CONSULTANT)

1. TERM
2. SERVICES

The Consultant is obliged to:

Carry out the training programmes and/or content development tasks on behalf of the Company as planned and mutually confirmed, and as per the dates and times mutually agreed to by the Company and the Consultant.

Make himself/herself available on telephone for a Train-the-Trainer session for the module at a prescheduled time that is agreed in advance by both i.e. the Consultant and the Company.

Ensure that all necessary preparations and prework are undertaken prior to the TTT and the delivery of the training programme.

Develop training modules for training when requested by the Company and agreeable to the Consultant, based on mutually agreed to compensation for the same.

Complete all training support tasks (e.g. collecting and mailing participant feedback and attendance to ABC) in a timely manner (within two business days of the training) and in the formats specified by Company. Failure to collect feedback from participants will result in fees being withheld for the training.

Refrain from using phone (to make or receive calls or messages) during the workshop delivery, even when participants are involved in activities. Calls/messages should be restricted to mid-morning/mid-afternoon tea and lunch breaks.

Execute the entrusted work in a highly professional, competent, and dignified manner.

Ensure appropriate grooming and business attire when conducting a training session or attending a Client meeting.

For men, the attire would be a formal shirt and trousers, (tie and jacket optional), shoes and socks (no jeans, t-shirts or sandals).

For women, formal western wear or Indian attire in non-flashy colours and prints (no capris, sleeveless clothing, flashy jewellery or slippers).

Arrive at the training location at least 30 minutes prior to the start of the programme to set up for the session, and greet participants as they arrive for the workshop.

Serve as a professional representative of the Company at the Client location. Consultant must not promote his/her independent brand or any third-party brand when interacting with Clients and their representatives. The Company is obliged to:

Provide training material to the Consultants in advance to give them adequate time to prepare for the TTT and the final delivery.

Supply Consultants with well-designed, error-free content which would not require any addition or modification.

Ensure that training material includes appropriate

trainer guides/notes, PowerPoint presentations, handouts for activities, feedback forms, exercise sheets, games, videos or any other material that is required to conduct the workshop.

Include information of participant profiles and Client objectives.

Reimburse any incidental expenses (e.g. outstation travel, stay, photocopying, courier) as confirmed in advance by the Company, except local conveyance and food expenses.

3. DESIGNATION

   The Consultant shall be designated as "Consultant" with the Company.

4. CONSIDERATION

   The COMPANY agrees to pay the Consultant as follows:

Training Assignments

For out-of-city assignments: The travel and accommodation costs for out-of-city assignments will be borne by the Company as per actual costs incurred by the Consultant, and approved by the Company. An additional sum of Rs 1,000/- per day all inclusive will be paid for out-of-city assignments over and above the local assignment rates. The following costs, however, will need to be borne by the Consultant:

a. Local transportation to and from airport/railway station/ bus stand if not reimbursed by the third-party Client.
b. Any meals costs incurred en route to out-of-city locations.
c. Dinner costs at out-of-city locations (in cases where it is not provided by the client).

The financial terms indicated in this contract are valid for the current financial year, and will renew automatically for the next financial year unless either party requests an amendment in the rates. No further negotiation regarding the terms, conditions and commercials will be entertained during the current financial Year. All rate amendment requests must be made in writing to ABC between February and March of the current financial year for the next financial year. No extra fee will be paid for any Train-the-Trainer session attended by the Consultant.

The payment for Training shall be made by the Company within 30–60 days from the date of the receipt of the Consultant's invoice for a programme that has been run. The payment will be made subject to the tasks being completed as assigned by the Company, as well as the required training materials and feedback forms being returned within 48 hours of completing the training programme.

The above amounts shall be paid to the Consultant after tax deduction at source (TDS) as applicable under the Income Tax Act 1961.

Post training, should the Client impose any penalty on the Company citing bad feedback from the participants or poor quality of programme delivery, the Company reserves the right to impose a financial penalty on the Consultant. Based on participant feedback collected by the Client (which will be shared with the Consultant), the penalty could be up to 50% of the Consultant's remuneration.

5. CONFIDENTIALITY

   The Consultant shall keep strictly confidential all information, documentation, etc. regarding the Company and its Clients which comes to his/her attention in the course of performing services for the Company. Such information shall not be disclosed to any third party or be used in whole or part for his personal benefit, without the company's prior permission in writing (except as required by applicable law, regulation or legal process).

   All financial arrangements between the Company and the Consultant are strictly confidential and must not be shared with the Client, other consultants working with the Company, or with competitive training agencies.

   The above confidentiality clauses will apply for one year after the termination of this agreement.

6. INDEMNITY: THE CONSULTANT WILL INDEMNIFY

THE COMPANY AS UNDER:

I will exercise utmost diligence in keeping confidential all confidential and proprietary information concerning Client of the Company and the Company itself which I may acquire during the course of my provision of consulting services to the Company. I will use such materials and information solely for the benefit of the Company and its Clients and will not use such information for any other entities or persons. At the conclusion of my relationship with the Company, I will return all confidential material and any copies thereof.

I will at all times exercise discretion in discussing with others the affairs of the Company and its Clients, avoiding unnecessary identification of names, places, and other specifics.

I agree to disclose and assign promptly all information, materials, products, and deliverables developed by me that is commissioned and paid for by the Company while acting as a consultant to the Company, and agree that the same shall be the exclusive property of the Company and all title and interest therein shall vest in the Company. Pursuant to its exclusive proprietary rights, the Company shall have the sole and exclusive right inter alia to use, modify or adapt the information, materials, products or deliverables that I developed during the performance of services as a consultant to the Company. I agree to provide all necessary assistance required to perfect such assignment of rights defined in this provision.

I will not, for a period of one year after the termination of this agreement, directly or indirectly solicit to provide, or provide without the prior written consent of the Company, any professional services such as those provided by the Company for any Client of the Company for whom I have provided services anytime during the previous twelve months. Further, the non-compete provisions will apply to any Client of the Company for whom I have performed services or with whom I have had significant professional contact over a period of twelve months prior to joining the Company and that the onus of informing the Company of any such association lies solely on me.

If I am directed by any government agency or judicial forum or asked to testify concerning any matter learned in the course of services provided to or on behalf of the Company, I will immediately notify the Company and will not voluntarily disclose such information to anyone without the prior consent of the Company.

That in the event I am found to be in breach of this agreement, I shall be liable to pay to the company a sum equivalent to the remuneration/compensation received by me from the Company in the last three months immediately preceding termination.

That I will not make any reference of company/its clients in any electronic media publications, internet, professional networking sites etc.

That I recognize that any material provided by the Company to me for the purpose of training their Clients is the exclusive property of the Company, and will not be used by me independent of the Company or shared with a third party without a written letter of consent from the Company.

7. COPYRIGHT

The copyright in all the works, training modules, training material, etc. commissioned by the Company and developed by the Consultant for the Company in exchange for a fee shall vest in the Company and all the course materials, slides, transparencies, etc. shall be the property of the Company. The consultant may not use such material for any training independent of the Company, and may not share such material with the Client or its representatives, or any independent third party individual or agency. This provision will be applicable even after termination of this agreement.

Any non-commissioned material developed by the Consultant and used by the Company for an agreed fee per usage shall be deemed the property of the Consultant and shall not be used independently by the Company.

8. TERMINATION OF AGREEMENT

Either party can terminate this agreement by giving a one-month notice in writing to the other party.

In case of a breach of the terms of this agreement by any party, the other party shall give a notice for rectifying the breach, and in case the breach is not rectified within seven days of the notice, this agreement shall stand terminated.

9. INDEPENDENT CONSULTANT

The Consultant is independent and is being engaged by the Company only for the purposes specified above, and there is no Master-Servant, Employer-Employee, or Principle-agent relationship between the parties hereto. The Consultant is free to offer services independently to any organization, provided it is not an organization for which he is already providing services through the Company. The Consultant is also free to decline any project offered by the Company without providing any reason for this. However, once a project offered by the Company is accepted by the Consultant, he/she may not subsequently decline the project.

10. MODIFICATION AND WAIVER

A modification or waiver of any of the provisions of this Agreement shall be effective only if made in writing and executed with the same formality as this Agreement.

11. SETTLEMENT OF DISPUTES

If any dispute or difference shall at any time arise between the Parties to this Agreement, or in any clause or their respective rights, claims or liabilities hereunder, or otherwise in any manner whatsoever, in relation to or arising out of or concerning this Agreement, the Parties shall promptly and in good faith negotiate with a view to its amicable resolution and settlement. In the event no amicable resolution or settlement is reached within a period of thirty (30) days from the date on which the dispute or difference arose, such dispute or difference shall be referred to sole Arbitrator who shall be appointed by the Company. The arbitration proceedings shall be held in Bangalore, India, as per the Arbitration and Conciliation Act, 1996, and any modifications thereto.

B: Sample Résumé

AN INNOVATIVE & ACCOMPLISHED TRAINING CONSULTANT

Six Sigma Lean & Green Belt Trained and Trained Trainer by the British Council of India, with 12 years of rich experience including nearly 3 years in delivering trainings for leading MNCs on Soft Skills and Communication skills

Initial 8 years' experience in Operations Account Management and Process Management in the ITES industry

PROFILE SUMMARY

- Specialization in:
    - Organizing diverse trainings such as Behavioural Trainings, Soft Skills Trainings, Motivational Trainings, Orientation Programme for new joiners, Internal Development Programme for staff promotion, etc.
    - Delivering trainings on topics such as Leadership, Team Building, Performance Development, Management

Development, Stress Management, Business Process Management, Culture Sensitization, E-Mail Etiquettes, Time Management, Conflict Management, Coaching & Mentoring, Report Writing etc.

PERSONALITY TRAITS

- Proficient in bringing transformation in people to adopt new ways of working; skilled in translating employee development behaviours into learning designs.
- Acquired experience in operations management, process management and service delivery, with experience in improving quality and escalating operational efficiency.
- Self-motivated with excellent planning, interpersonal & leadership skills; ability to interact easily with people of diverse backgrounds, cultures, and professional levels.

CORE COMPETENCIES

- Devising & implementing training strategy; analysing business needs and learning needs; taking decisions on why a training programme is seen as the recommended solution to a business problem.
- Identifying training incumbents and their level of existing knowledge on the subject; undertaking an

KEY SKILLS

analysis of the tasks performed and job requirements; analysing documents, laws, procedures used on the job; ensuring that the training content does not contradict job requirements.

- Preparing the training programme calendar; establishing training materials and outlining effective instructional methods; evaluating training feedback and analysing Return on Investment (ROI) of training.
- Managing operations with accountability of development of effective plans for achievement of SLA & quality norms; ensuring timely delivery of multiple projects as per requirements of compliance, quality, time and cost parameters; re-designing business processes to achieve strategic goals.
- Handling new process launches with accountability of analysis of data exchange layouts, data transfer, reporting and communication with the internal/external team; monitoring process with respect to AHT, TAT, etc. Ensuring compliance to the laid guidelines (IOPs and SOPs).
- Building strong rapport with customers through customer centric approach; maintaining cordial relations with customers to sustain the profitability of the business.

FREELANCE EXPERIENCE

Since Dec'12 serving as Freelance Corporate Trainer (Soft skills and Behavioral skills) with various MNCs

Accomplishments:

- Holds the distinction of developing & implementing trainings on Soft skills & Communication skills, such as:

  Campus to Corporate

Reliance Industries, Capricorn Logistics, Minda Corporation, Jindal Steel

Cognizant, JP Morgan Chase, Thomson Reuters, FirstSource, SDL Multilingual, AltiSource

Kaizen Technologies Pvt. Ltd, C-DAC (Center for Development of Advanced Computing)

Walchand Institute of Technology, St. Angelo's Professional Education

KEY CLIENTS HANDLED

Leadership, Team Building, Performance Development, Outbound programmes
- Creative Problem Solving, Management Development, Stress Management, Goal Setting
- Business Process Management, Culture Sensitization, E-Mail Etiquette, Time Management, Conflict Management
- Change Management, Competency Based Interviewing, Coaching & Mentoring
- Customer Relationship Management, Customer Service
- Advance Excel and PowerPoint Presentation

- Developed content and Delivered trainings for high profile clients such as:
    - Reliance Industries, Capricorn Logistics, Kumar Constructions, A.T.E. Enterprises, Minda Corporation, Jindal Steel, SBI Bank
    - E-Next Financial Services, Cognizant, JP Morgan Chase, Thomson Reuters, FirstSource, SDL Multilingual, AltiSource, Ocwen
    - Let's Talk (Center for Communication Skills and Finishing Skills), Mukesoft IT Consultants
    - Apex Consumer Appliances, Kaizen Technologies Pvt. Ltd, C-DAC (Center for Development of Advanced Computing)
    - Walchand Institute of Technology, St. Angelo's Professional Education, UFaber.com

CAREER GRAPH

C: Sample Trainer Profile—One-Pager

Amit Joshi
Training Consultant, India

Coach's Overview:
Amit Joshi is an innovative and accomplished Training consultant and comes with an overall experience of 13+ years in Language and Soft skills Training, Profit Centre Operations, and Account Management. He has facilitated and coached clients from various industries through diverse trainings.

He is a trained trainer for English Communication skills by the British Council and has been recognized for creating stimulating and interactive learning environments, encouraging participation and individual creativity. In addition to this, Amit improvises the content to suit the experience level and knowledge level of trainees. He has a Bachelor's degree in Engineering (Instrumentation).

Representative Client Engagements:

- Imparted training programmes across various industries

like Information Technology, ITES, Manufacturing, Power, Logistics, Engineering, Construction as well as Education at Entry and Mid Management levels in India.

- Trained Client employees on Management development, Presentation Skills, Business Communication, Accent Neutralization, Accent Enhancement, Language Lab, Email Etiquette, Telephone Etiquette, Report writing, Campus to Corporate Programmes, Business Etiquette, Culture Sensitization and many more.

Representative Clients:

- FirstSource
- Jindal Steel
- JP Morgan
- E-Next
- Cognizant Technology Solutions
- ATE Engineering
- Thomson Reuters
- Walchand Inst. of Technology
- Reliance Power
- C-DAC, Pune
- Capricorn Logistics

Education:

- B.E. (Instrumentation)

Certifications:

- Train the Trainer, Bodhih
- Instructional design, Tata Institute of Social Sciences
- English Communication skills, British Council
- Entrepreneurship Development, NIESBUD
- Kaizen Certification (Yellow Belt) Project on "Risk Mitigation Through Process Automation" at Maersk GSC.
- Advance Excel, SMU

D: Sample Cover Letter

Hi ________,

With reference to your post on LinkedIn regarding the requirement for Freelance Trainers, I would love to be interviewed for this position.

I am a Trained Trainer by the British Council of India, with over 13 years of rich experience in Training, Operations Management, and Account Management. I have trained over 1700 participants and have over 2500 hours of training experience with leading MNCs for Soft skills and Behavioural skills. I have attached my resume/profile for your reference.

I would love to further discuss my credentials with you. You can call me on 98__________ to discuss.

Regards,

Amit Joshi

Corporate Trainer

Behavioral skills/Soft skills

Mob: __________________

Note: Through this letter, you are not only expressing your keen interest for the role, you are very clearly expressing your expectation, that is, to discuss further by mentioning it a couple of times and also providing your contact details at two places. This particular format has worked for me with a good success rate.

Another variation of the same letter is shown here:

I would love to be interviewed for the position of ____________

Hi ________,

With reference to our LinkedIn conversation, attached is my resume for your reference.

I am a Trained Trainer by the British Council of India, with over 13 years of rich experience in Training, Operations Management, and Account Management. I have trained over 1700 participants and have over 2500 hours of training experience with leading MNCs for Soft skills and Behavioural skills.

I would love to further discuss my credentials with you. You can call me on_________ to discuss.

Regards,

Amit Joshi

Corporate Trainer

Behavioural skills/Soft skills

Mob: ________________

This format, in addition to clearly stating your expectation, helps you to stand out from the other applicants, thereby increasing the chances of getting a favourable response. I have myself used this format several times and got a good response.

E: Sample Proposal

Objective: To enhance Communication Skills of the participants through an online programme

Summary of our discussion on 19 June

- There is a need for an online training programme on Communication skills as most of the participants are busy and would find it convenient to take an online course rather than classroom training.
- We need to assess the current Reading, Writing, Listening, and Speaking skills with more importance to Reading and Writing.
- The assessment needs to be as per IELTS standards (International English Language Testing System).
- Amit Joshi shared an alternative way of assessing the candidates for the grammatical proficiency directly on the basis of tests.
- The system should be able to track the progress of the participants and also motivate them to complete the module on time.

- Amit Joshi to provide a demo of the online module along with the Assessment parameters, Reporting and Sample training modules before 25 June.
- Amit Joshi to also provide a quotation for the module for about 30–35 participants.

PROPOSAL

We wish to partner with your organization to train the candidates in Communication skills through an online programme. The programme will include a Pre-assessment to gauge the current proficiency level of the participants and a Post-assessment to track the improvement through the programme.

We would design content to deliver a specific programme targeted at the participants to help them improve their communication skills i.e. Reading, Writing, and Speaking skills.

(A) Programme Customisation and Design

The participants get an opportunity to enhance their Communication skills through an effective online programme. Effective learning in a domain like Communication skills is dependent on several factors including learning methodology, content design &development, trainer quality, consistent tracking & feedback apart from a personal touch. We own the complete responsibility of the entire delivery of the programme.

(B) Programme Delivery Plan

- We will deliver a customized 45 hour programme that will include a Pre and Post training assessment and Communication skills training module, details of which are mentioned below.
- The programme will be designed and executed by Amit Joshi (profile appended below).

Programme outline

INTRODUCTION

Everything rises and falls on the effectiveness of communication. Communication has the ability to confuse, clarify, encourage, instruct or teach. Hence it is vital to sharpen one's communication skills to enhance overall effectiveness.

OBJECTIVES

To provide an overview of the basic concepts of Grammar to enhance communication skills and to improve Email Writing skills of the participants. To equip the participants with the techniques and skills required to communicate effectively in Business settings.

COURSE CONTENT

- Grammar Tenses: Present tense and its forms, Future tense and forms, Past tense and its forms
- Subject-Verb agreement
- Use of Articles
- Prepositions
- Sentence Construction
- Types of sentences

Programme Cost

The entire programme will cost Rs ____ /- per participant with a minimum 30 Learners. The cost includes the following:

- Detailed Pre and Post Assessment with feedback.
- Comprehensive online course with practice assignments with 24/7 access and downloadable content.

F: Sample Programme Outline

Selling skills training

Conducted by

Amit Joshi

INTRODUCTION

Selling skills are critical in organizations that rely on ongoing buying from customers or clients. The ability to build relationships with customers, persuade them to make purchases and generate repeat business is at the heart of selling.

OBJECTIVES

By the end of this workshop, the participants will be able to:

- Describe the call flow for an Outbound sales call
- Describe the importance of Non-verbal communication
- Identify the difference between Features, Advantages, and Benefits
- Demonstrate how to handle objections from customers,
- Identify the elements of a good sales call

CONTENTS

- Importance of selling skills
- Outbound call flow—Introduction, Main body, Conclusion
- Importance of Non-verbal communication—Tone, pitch, pace, pause, energy
- FAB—Features, Advantages Benefits
- Objection Handling—LAMA model
- Skills required to be a successful salesperson
- Active listening skills
- Acknowledgement, Paraphrasing
- Steering the conversation—Questioning techniques
- Traits of a successful salesperson
- Ways of engaging your customers
- Self-fulfilling prophecy
- Staying motivated
- Elements of a good sales call
- Role plays and mock calls

DURATION

1 day

METHODOLOGY

PowerPoint Presentations, Classroom Training, Group Discussions, Examples, Exercises, Games Fun-Learning Activities, and Visuals.

G: Sample Invoice

Bill To:

Company name and address

Invoice No.: 01

Please make checks payable to:

Bank Details:

Name:______________________

Account No.:____________________

Bank:______________________

Branch:_____________________

IFSC:______________________

PAN:______________________

Date:__________

SN	DESCRIPTION	RATE	TOTAL
1	Programme Name -	----------------	----------------
2	Other charges - Stationery, printing, props etc.	----------------	----------------
		TOTAL	----------------

____
(Trainer's signature)

____
Trainer name

If you have any questions concerning this invoice, please contact

Amit joshi ____________(mobile no.)

THANK YOU FOR YOUR BUSINESS!

H: Sample Introductory LinkedIn Messages

Hi ,
I am Amit B Joshi, Trainer for Soft Skills and Behavioural Skills and have trained over 2500 participants from leading MNCs. Is grooming your workforce on these areas, on the horizon for your business at this point? If so, may I propose a short email exchange — to discuss further? Please let me know.
Thanks for your time.
Amit B Joshi
Corporate Trainer
Soft Skills & Behavioural Skills
Mob no.

Hi ,
I am a Trainer for Soft Skills and Behavioural Skills, and have trained over 2500 participants from leading MNCs. Are you empanelling Trainers in these areas at this point? If so, would love to collaborate with your organisation. Please suggest how we can work together for mutual benefit.
Thanks for your time.
Regards,
Amit B Joshi
Corporate Trainer
Soft skills & Behavioural skills
Mob no.

Additional Reading

Books:
Bozart, Jane, *Social Media for Trainers.*
Dib, Allan, *The 1-Page Marketing Plan: Get New Customers, Make More Money, and Stand Out*, From The CrowdKindle Edition.
Habegger, Leonardo, *How to Become the Leader in Your Niche: On Authority Positioning.*
Kiyosaki, Robert, *Rich Dad Poor Dad.*
Norris, Dan, *Content Machine: Use Content Marketing to Build a 7-figure Business With Zero Advertising*, Kindle Edition.
Wilkinson, Bruce, *Seven Laws of the Learner*

Online Resources:
The Future of Learning: http://www.learninggeneralist.com/2010/05/changing-our-trainer-mindsets.html
Six hats of a Trainer: http://www.learninggeneralist.com/2010/01/six-hats-of-trainer.html
Mindset—Carol S. Dweck Reference for Presentation skills training:http://www.speakingaboutpresenting.com/presentation-skills/presentation-skills-trainer/
http://vnutravel.typepad.com/trainingday/2006/08/its_all_about_a.html

Note from the Publisher

Dear Reader,

We hope this book has been useful to you and has provided you with expert information related to a freelance training career. This book contains material that you would require in making a decision about a career in freelance training or as a new entrant in this field. However, in order to assist you with more in-depth information about this subject, a QR code that links to **Digital Resources** has been given below. Through these resources you will be able to see videos where the author clarifies several concepts and provides more detailed information. You will also be able to download a soft copy of some content from the book.

How to use the QR code:
Download any QR code scanner app from your app store on your mobile and then scan the QR code given below.

Thank you for choosing this book!

About Indus Source Books

Indus Source Books is a niche, independent book publisher in Mumbai passionately committed to publishing good and relevant literature. We believe that books are one of the most important mediums of communication and we seek to bring out publications that help to serve the community and the world we live in.

At Indus Source Books, we celebrate the diverse spiritual traditions, culture, and history of the world and present it to our readers in a contemporary format that retains its essential flavour: "Indian Spirit, Universal Wisdom".

Visit our website www.indussource.com for more details.

Indus Source Books
PO Box 6194
Malabar Hill PO
Mumbai 400006
India
www.indussource.com
info@indussource.com